ROTOMA
The ROI of Social Media
'Top of Mind'

Spencer X. Smith & D.P. Knudten

ROTOMA–The ROI of Social Media 'Top of Mind'

ISBN: 978-1973879954

Book cover & interior design:
D.P. Knudten / COLLABORATOR Publications

PRINTED IN THE U.S.A.

I'd like to dedicate this book to all the many, many wonderful people who have motivated and inspired me over the years. There are too many of you to name individually, and for fear of omitting one (or many) of you, I'll simply say, "Thank you." You know who you are.

- Spencer X. Smith

To Elizabeth, the woman who inexplicably saw potential, and continues to polish the rock hoping for something shiny.

- D.P. Knudten

CONTENTS

An Introduction–literally.

Nick Lombardino of Atlas Providers is one of those 'Connector' types Malcolm Gladwell wrote about in *The Tipping Point*. He knows, and connects, just about everyone who is anybody in Madison's startup space with an open heart that expects nothing in return. He's a pure 'sharer' for sure. So when I found myself needing to do a little bit of a professional pivot, the first person I called was Nick.

"Have you met Spencer X. Smith?," he asked after a few minutes of small talk.

"No, I haven't, but I've seen the guy's work all over the place. The man is a social media monster," said I.

And he is, plugged into every viable, valuable social media channel there is. He's also another Gladwellian Connector / Giver. Nick gave me Spencer's contact info, and I took it from there.

We met. I swam through an avalanche of Spencer's hard-earned knowledge, and we immediately became fast friends. His point-of-view re: social sharing blew me away. The depth of his insight, so freely shared, was near astounding. Simply put, the guy's a giver, with a heck of a lot to give.

When he later asked if I'd be interested in writing a book with him, the answer was an immediate 'yes.' The central concept, ROTOMA (aka The Return on Top of Mind Awareness) made sense to me instantly as an incredibly elegant explanation for the 'why do it' of social media. Every good salesman has long known that the best way to make a sale is to make a friend first. And that's exactly what social media enables you to do—for FREE.

So here we are. ROTOMA has gone from 'what if' to bound book. Like any conversation with Spencer, there's a lot here, and even more to digest. A couple notes re: housekeeping. Both Spencer and I are first-person, 'write what you know' types. With both of us bouncing back and forth, adding comments and content throughout the book, that could get a little confusing on the 'who said what front.'

With that in mind, in editing this book I tried to retain our distinctive voices by taking an anthology approach throughout. You'll be able to track who authored the original section 'soup stock' by simply looking for the profile pic next to the section title, but know that we both added a little of our own personal blend of herbs & spices to each other's original recipe.

This is Spencer.   This is me.

Another tell: If it's earnest, about the band Myopic Son, or clearly from a salesman's point of view, it's Spencer. If it's got a touch of attitude, is overly fond of intra-section subheads, and clearly coming from the mind or mouth of an advertising copywriter & Creative Director, it's me.

Write what you know, and in your own voice. We both did—and really hope you get something out of it.

- D.P. Knudten, Madison, Wisconsin / August, 2017

ROTOMA

The ROI of Social Media
'Top of Mind'

The #1 social media metric no one is talking about.

My friend, a brilliant attorney named Erin Ogden of OgdenGlazer, LLC in Madison, recently told me this story:

"I saw another attorney today at lunch who I hadn't seen in awhile. He said, 'Oh, Erin! I am going to be sending a client your way. It is a friend of a friend who I think will fit with you well.' Now, did he already make that connection prior to lunch? Probably, knowing him. But now the thought has solidified and the push to follow up is more present than before. Did it 'get' me the original thought for referral? No. But it got it closer to actually happening. And I have found that once you get one referral from someone, you get more. **You become more entrenched as top-of-mind.***"*

Top of mind. What a powerful yet nebulous term. In my estimation, 'top of mind' is really a lesson in associations. The smell of a campfire is something you may associate with summer nights, while the sound of a whistle may remind you of a particularly good coach (or one who made you run when you messed up—thanks Coach Damron). In Erin's case, an attorney saw her and it triggered the "referral for Erin" association.

Top of mind.
What a powerful, yet often under-played,
benefit of social media.

There's one question I hear more than any other when designing digital and social media campaigns for prospective customers: **"What's my ROI?"** (Return on Investment)

How often have you asked yourself this question in relation to your online business activities?

How often have you tried, in vain, to calculate your return on investment in digital and social media? Has it led to apathy? Or worse yet, a negative association altogether?

Can this stuff really work? Can social media really help me in my business? **The answer is yes, because of the one social media metric no one is talking about.**

First off though, let's go back to 2008.

I had a sales job (um, I mean I was regional sales director, and later a regional vice president) that required travel from Madison to Indianapolis. I'd work in Indianapolis starting Monday morning, stay there during the workweek to visit customers and prospective customers, and return to Madison on Friday evening.

Challenge No. 1
Madison is in the Central time zone. And Indianapolis? The Eastern time zone. In other words, you lose an hour driving to Indy and gain that hour back on the way to Madison. Because my typical Monday meetings would start in Indianapolis at 9 a.m., I would leave Madison at 2:30 a.m. to make it on time.

Challenge No. 2
You're driving on Monday mornings from Madison to Indianapolis. What do you do in the car during that time? Listen to music? Audiobooks? Foreign language instructionals? I did all of those things. After a few weeks of the same Monday morning routine over and over, I realized I was wasting a lot of time. "I should really make phone calls," I thought to myself.

Challenge No. 3
Is it socially acceptable to make phone calls before 8 a.m. Central time on a Monday morning? Nope. Don't ever do that. Trust me.

Here's what I discovered though. It was okay to call people at their place of business, if I knew they wouldn't be there. "What's the point of that?" you may be asking yourself.

This is the point: During that five-and-a-half hours in the car, I was able to leave almost 200 voicemail messages. I wouldn't just leave voicemails to follow up, check in, or touch base. You know, those terms we so often use when we just want to ask someone, "Are you ready to buy yet or not?"

Instead, I'd tell stories via these messages to highlight what was happening in my industry. I'd share thoughts on what I saw working well, what I saw not working well, and what my prospective or actual customers could learn from my experience in the sales field.

Nobody answers office calls at 5 a.m.– and that's a good thing.

I left those voicemails knowing two things:

1. Customers and prospective customers, arriving at their offices on Monday morning, would press a button to listen to their voicemail and they'd hear my voice.

2. Customers and prospective customers would be reminded of me as a result of hearing my voice.

For any of us working in business, there's a huge difference between someone thinking about you and someone not thinking about you. To use a term from biology, there is virtual half-life related to this fact. As the chasm between 'not thinking about you' and 'thinking about you' grows, the less and less likely it is that someone will consider you and your business at the right time.

During my long Monday-morning drives, the voicemails I'd leave—from a very binary standpoint—could be summed up in two regards:

1. Either I left those voicemails or I didn't. I'd use time productively or simply waste it.

2. Either my customers and prospective customers were thinking about me or they weren't.

As easy as it was for me to leave these voicemail messages, it was equally as easy for me not to do it.

I really had no idea which voicemail had impact and which didn't. But if I didn't take those actions, though, I had absolutely zero chance of maintaining top-of-mind awareness. At least these voicemails gave me a chance. Without the activity I had zero return, while with the activity I at least had a hope of some return on my time investment in the form of 'top of mind' presence in those customers' minds.

Guess what happened?

It wasn't necessarily the Monday morning I'd leave those voicemails, nor the Monday after that, or even the Monday after that one, but eventually, I'd hear back from these customers and prospective customers. They'd say, "You know, Spence, a few months ago you shared a story, and I'm running into a similar situation now. What was that story again?"

These people, with whom I was trying to stay top-of-mind, would ask me for help as a consultant, not as a salesperson. They would ask for my assistance very, very early in the sales cycle, and not near the end when I would compete based on price or another commodity.

Let's consider this same situation when it comes to your social media.

How difficult is it to post something on social media? About as easy as something gets, right? You type some words, add an image if appropriate, and hit publish, post, or share. How easy is it not to post on social media? Equally as easy, right? There are no looming deadlines or demands.

There's a major difference between my voicemails and our social media shares though: scale.

Think about this; it would take me over a half a working day to reach fewer than 200 people in 2008, and now you can reach hundreds (or possibly thousands) of people in minutes.

**Let me repeat that—
it's possible for you to reach thousands of people
in minutes, even seconds, via social media.**

Back to my friend Erin:

"Social media can be both a vehicle to get me in front of people through posts and showing that I am a source of knowledge, but it can also help me find things to use to reach out to people. I am a content provider so I get people mentioning my posts quite often, but even as a content consumer it can help me find a topic for an email, phone call, or even an in-person chat about something other than the weather."

What Erin said is key for two reasons:

1. Social media can first be used to listen. Find out what people are talking about before saying something.

2. Being a content provider (and not just a consumer) is the key method for maintaining top-of-mind awareness.

An idea this powerful deserves its own acronym: ROTOMA

If ROI = Return on Investment, and I invested time to become 'top of mind' with my customers, what I'm really looking for is a **r**eturn **o**n my investment to achieve '**t**op **of m**ind' **a**wareness with my customers. ***Eureka…err…ROTOMA!***

Instead of worrying about the ROI of social media, concentrate on something much more simple: ROTOMA.

How can you maximize your own ROTOMA?

Stop spending your time sending emails or voicemails to follow up, check in, or touch base. Remember, those terms we so often use when we just want to ask someone, "Are you ready to buy yet or not?" Instead, tell stories through social media (as well as through email and voicemail) to highlight what's happening in your industry. Share your thoughts on what's working well, what's not working well, and what your customer or prospective customer can learn from your experience.

Either you're communicating on social media or you're not. Either you're top-of-mind with someone or you're not. Share your experiences and share your wisdom, and watch your ROTOMA through social media soar.

✝

Success on social isn't mathematical. It's biological.

I like to start many of my presentations by asking the audience for their reaction to this statement: Social media is more biological than mathematical.

They immediately make the connection. "When you're posting and interacting on social media, you are interacting with people," they answer.

You may have read a dozen "How To" articles about cracking the algorithms—which sound very mathematical—of any social media platform, but at the end of the day, you're communicating with people.

And as people, social media users are prone to one very natural, very biological tendency: They forget things. They forget people.

Memories have a biological half life. If someone sees you or something you post, there might be a 50 percent chance that they'll think about you during the next week. The second week? Maybe a 25 percent chance. The likelihood of your connections thinking about you drops dramatically from the point when you last communicated with them, unless you give them a new reason to think about you.

At any given moment, you can be sure of one thing: Either your prospective clients are thinking about you or they're not thinking about you. Well, duh. But think about it. If they're not thinking about you, there's a 0 percent chance that they're going to call you when they face a problem.

Social media is a great way to make your clients think about you.

Before social media, this was a lot harder. I used to work in sales for a Fortune 100 company before social media had taken off. I lived in Madison, but my first sales territory was Indiana. Eventually I graduated to Chicago, and finally I got home to Wisconsin. I kept the same phone number with each jump. I had made a habit of calling my clients regularly, and through my time in each territory I developed many working relationships.

But each time I moved on to the next territory, I rarely, if ever, heard from those connections again. My contact info was the same, but since I wasn't calling them, they forgot about me. Since we didn't have social media, the only way for me to contact them would be to use work time that was reserved for my current territory, or to use my personal time that was reserved for my family and personal friends. Had social media existed back then, it would have been a lot easier to maintain those business relationships.

Social media offers you the chance to
become famous within your field.
All you have to do is be consistent.

When I was a kid, if you had asked me to name five famous people, I probably would have listed a few actors, a few major league baseball players, and the president of the United States. And a lot of people my age would have named the same celebrities.

At the time, the number of people who could become famous was finite. Either you were an actor, a professional athlete, or you were a politician.

But now, we have micro-celebrities. Ask a hundred 12-year-olds who their favorite YouTuber is, and you'll get a hundred different answers.

Because of social media, you don't have to become famous in the traditional sense—CEO of a Fortune 500 company, NBA player, movie star—before you start impacting people that you've never met.

Social media gives you a path to earn fame by producing great content, consistently.

Everyone thinks, "Why me?" My answer: "Why not you?"

Have you heard of the 1 percent rule of the internet? Here it is. internet users are divided into three categories. You're going to recognize yourself in one of them.

- **90 percent of users are only observers and silent consumers.**
  They read, watch, listen, laugh, cry, but they don't engage.

- **9 percent of users engage.**
  They like, comment, and share.

- **1 percent of users create.**
  They share of themselves via original content.

Which category do you fall in?

Let's talk about that 10 (9 + 1) percent.

If you put something out on the internet, and you track the engagement metrics because you're obsessed with knowing the ROI of your effort, you can only ever track 10 percent of your potential impact!

If you know there are people out there watching, even though they're not engaging, it's incumbent on you to keep serving them, knowing that they're watching.

The first excuse I hear as to why someone is not on social media is that no one is listening. **What's the point? What's the ROI?** But think about your own behavior. How many posts, conversations, videos and tweets do you read without engaging at all? People are listening, and simply by creating content, you have the opportunity to distinguish yourself as part of the 1 percent.

The key to hacking the biological platform of social media is consistency.

It's better to provide snippets of value every few days than to let months go by between posts. It goes back to that biological half life. Think about binge watching a show on Netflix. When Netflix releases a whole season of Orange is the New Black at once, everyone talks about it for a week. They're obsessed with the complex story lines and characters. But three months later, while waiting for the next season to be produced, nobody is thinking about Piper.

All it takes for you to stay at the top of your connections' mind on social media is to post valuable content consistently.

There's no mathematical formula, just human nature.

ROTOMA is all about leveraging that basic human nature as efficiently as possible. And that's what social media is: the most efficient and powerful top-of-mind awareness toolset in the history of the world. And 90+% of it is FREE to use. All it takes is a little time, an open mind, and the willingness to get out of your own way.

So what's stopping you?

The most powerful ROTOMA tool? Asking a question.

Here's a short, and completely true, story about how one question led to the career I have today. It's a wonderful example of a recurring theme you'll notice throughout this book; the real 'top of mind' power of not having the answer, but in asking good questions, and then acting on the answers you receive.

Since 1999, Milwaukee's Summerfest has been recognized by Guinness World Records as the world's largest annual music festival. Over 700 bands perform during the 11-day event each year, and some of the most popular artists in the world have played on one of its 11 stages.

As a kid growing up in Milwaukee, I dreamed I was one of the rock stars on that stage, entertaining the thousands of people in the audience. This dream actually came true in 2002 when my band, Myopic Son, which had only formed in 2000, had our first opportunity to play the 'Big Gig.'

As both the drummer and the booking manager, this was a huge accomplishment of which I'm still proud today. How did we do it? And what does this have to do with you and your business? Let's dive deep into how you can use the Summerfest Effect to build your brand.

Why it's so desirable
to perform at Summerfest.

Since Summerfest is the world's largest music festival, it's obviously one of the most sought-after places in the world to perform. There are some deeper reasons to consider, though, if you're managing and booking a rock band. Here are three:

1. It's very, very exclusive. Summerfest is run so incredibly well, and it's a different experience playing on a huge stage with such great sound. Our band performed on the second-largest stage on the grounds (capacity ~6000) and as a result, the fans we already had and the fans we earned during the performance saw (and heard) us in the best possible way. The experience, then, is unique and ultimately memorable for both our band and fans alike.

2. There are incredible networking opportunities. With 700 different bands coming through Milwaukee over 11 days, the bands themselves, their managers, their agents, and all of their support staff are available on-site. Since there are no rock band trade shows, this is as close as you can get to a rock Chamber of Commerce event.

3. Everyone wants to play in Milwaukee during the summer. Since those of us in the Midwest realize we have a finite period of outdoor time every year, all the great shows happen during the summer. Logistics for a band play a huge role in their touring schedule because of the sheer amount of people, gear, and merchandise that need to travel.

Once the Summerfest date is booked, the rest of the summer schedule can fill in around it. A Chicago show the day before, a Minneapolis show the day after, etc.

How our band booked the 'Big Gig.'

So how did our band get to perform at Summerfest?
I asked.

Yep, it's really as simple as that. Of course, we had to qualify in the minds of those responsible for booking us, but by asking, they gave us a step-by-step road map of what to do. From that road map, I developed a hierarchical pyramid, and starting at the bottom, worked our way up. As you move to each step, the peer group gets more and more rare and exclusive.

The Summerfest Effect

Milwaukee's Summerfest is one of the most sought after gigs in music. To book a slot, a band needs to be diligent and follow the steps outlined here. At each step, your peer group gets more rare and exclusive.

The same applies to your business. Dare to envision a big, daunting goal, be bold enough to ask how to get there, then take the steps necessary to achieve it.

- FORMAL PRESS KIT
- PRESS/MAGAZINE REVIEWS
- SELL TICKETS TO A SHOW
- RELEASE AN ALBUM
- RECORD A SONG
- WRITE A SONG
- PERFORM FOR A CROWD
- JOIN A BAND

To reach the top, you have to start at the bottom.

Here's the most interesting thing—when we approached the Summerfest's booking agent, she said something incredibly cool:

"I get approached by bands wanting to play here all the time.
What you asked, though, was different. You asked. 'What do we do to earn a spot at Summerfest?' Most bands just expect it to happen. They sign with a record label, and their manager calls wondering what time they'll play. Because you asked the way you did, I'll show you exactly how to earn it."

And she did.

Two major things she told us
I still use in business today.

• Don't assume anyone will ever give you anything because you think you deserve it. You need to find out what they want and help them get it.

• When you trust a third party to do your work on your behalf (like the band managers she mentioned), things will never go quite as well as if you did them. If it's critically important to the success of your endeavor, you just need to make the time to do it.

I'm convinced that many businesspeople—the band, in my mind, was the ultimate entrepreneurial endeavor & business—get in their own way a lot of the time. Because Summerfest is such a big deal, a lot of the other bands that we knew at the time simply didn't even try to play there. Why?

Although they would probably never admit it, *they might not have been good enough in their own minds.* The last part of that sentence is so important. Our band wasn't better than any of the other bands that we'd consider our peers. We were just bold (naive?) enough to expect to play at Summerfest if we asked the question and followed the advice we were given. That naiveté served us incredibly well in the success of our band. After all, why wouldn't someone want to hear the music we wrote?

The Summerfest Effect effect.

What happened after our band performed at Summerfest? Imagine you're a volunteer for a non-profit organization. Every year, your marquee event is a summer festival that raises the majority of the money from this one event. Depending on the size of the event, you might hire a promoter. Usually, though, booking bands falls squarely on the shoulders of one person with very little experience in this field.

This year, you are responsible for booking the bands. How do you go about doing this? You're staring at a calendar with a bunch of open time slots on it and wondering how the heck you're going to fill it.

Just as importantly, you don't want to make any mistakes and look stupid. What if you pick a band that isn't very good? Then you think to yourself, "You know what? Every band I've ever seen at Summerfest has been really great. Maybe I should start there."

This is what ended up happening to our band after Summerfest. Once our band had been vetted by Summerfest, no one needed to worry if we were good. When someone wasn't calling us, we were calling them to let them know we could help them check a box off of their to-do list.

Even if we didn't perform well —which fortunately never happened—the person responsible for booking us could say, "I'm not sure what happened, they played Summerfest, and that's a lot bigger event than our event."

After we put on a great show, then, we helped make that person feel good and look good to their peers. Isn't that what we're all trying to do in business?

Whether our customers are businesses or consumers:
people want to check off a task as "done,"
and feel good about it.

If this person is making a decision where their boss will ultimately hold them responsible, isn't looking good (i.e. not doing something that will get you fired) one of the most important goals?

How to use the Summerfest Effect to build your brand.

Here's what I propose you do to create your own Summerfest Effect: Find a big, daunting goal that would scare most people and find out how to do it. Don't stop until it's done or until you decide it isn't important anymore. If it doesn't scare you at least a little bit, then you're not thinking big enough.

Maybe it's speaking at a trade show or industry event. Maybe it's winning the business of a big-name client that most of your competitors would be scared to call. Maybe it's the book you could write from your experiences in your business. Think to yourself, "What could I do that would separate me most from my competition?"

For me, this challenge took the form of a keynote presentation gig. I really wanted to present at the Wisconsin Alumni Research Foundation meeting in January of 2015.

I asked the Director of Programming, "How can I help you book a great event and give a presentation answering questions your attendees have for you?"

By asking that question and acting immediately on her specific answers by developing a talk that served her purposes and her audience, I helped her solve some specific problems she had, and she rewarded me for it with a speaking slot.

The day of the event, before I even got on stage, several people came up and asked me, "So how did you get to do this?"

Simple. **I asked.**

Starting your own ROTOMA cover band.

I've seen Spencer speak numerous times, and like every ex-band dude, he always finds a way to weave stories from his Myopic Son glory days into just about every one of them. Not because he's a one-hit wonder, but because promoting a band has so many deep parallels with creating a successful social media strategy for yourself or your business.

You can read a number of lessons he's learned over the years throughout the book, but I wanted to add my $.02 from a slightly different point of view: the guy up front with the microphone.

As we were talking about the book and its contents, Spencer said something along the lines of "Dude, I was stuck behind a drum kit and never dealt with the audience directly, but given your background, you should totally talk about it. I bet you've got something to say." And he's right.

Long boring story short: years on stage doing improv comedy, pro acting, and folky singer/songwriting has given me a lot of experience dealing with audiences, most of which wish you'd just shut up so they could continue their conversations.

That sounds exactly like social media, amirite? Of course, if that audience actually paid money to see you because they want what you have to perform, that's another thing entirely—but I'm not talking about that situation.

I'm talking about trying to get some attention for something you've poured your heart into. Something that makes you feel vulnerable like never before. A precious, fragile thing you've sincerely crafted to share with anyone, everyone, who might possibly appreciate it. Yeah, that REALLY sounds like social media—and songwriting.

You have a voice. It's yours, and yours alone. And it deserves to be heard.

Not so long ago, everybody performed. Couldn't sing? You could recite poems, tells jokes, perform in skits. Then came radio, and performance became the domain of professionals, and everybody stopped performing themselves, becoming the passive consumer-only audiences of today. Well guess what, social media changed all that. In the words of Sager and Allen "Everything old is new again."

Here are some music lessons I'd like to add to Spencer's extensive list:

Write for your audience— it's bigger than you think.

Let's say you're an HR-compliance expert who really has a lot to say about inter-generation workforce issues. Back in the old days (pre-2000), you'd go to the single conference that exists to meet others in your area, learn a lot, then go home until next year's conference. Any thoughts or questions you might develop might have found a voice on some Usenet group or HR-related BBS, but that's about it.

Fast forward to now, and you can meet, converse, and share ideas with every single HR professional on the globe anywhere, and at anytime. Your audience may not be huge by Katy Perry standards (over 100MM Twitter fans at the time of this writing), but it could be legitimately said to be worldwide.

Writing what you know for your specific 'best' audience is the fastest way to build visibility, prestige, and expert credibility within your chosen area of expertise.

Collect Civil War buttons? Start blogging relevant, well researched content about them, then tweeting/Facebooking/et al to amplify your message, and you'll have armies of re-enactors descending on your piece of the internet. And the more specific you can be, the better.

Write what you want to say, not what you think they want to hear.

There is a ton of garbage out there masquerading as content. So much so, the word 'content' has been delegitimized and denigrated to 'that which fills the copy blocks in my layout' (see extended rant, *Killer Cereal*, on page 149.)

All of that clickbaity listicle, 'You won't believe what happened next!' bullroar threatens the very foundations of the web—but here's how you can help: **write quality content about anything you really know well.**

For all the shallow-end flotsam, there is still a ton of deep-end treasure to be had, and about every topic known to humankind. And you can add to it any time. The more you share your questions, your ideas, and your expertise the better that gold to crap ratio becomes.

By doing that, you add an original voice worth hearing. But just like 'overnight sensation' bands that spent ten years getting there, it doesn't happen overnight. Write like you think your future depends on it, because when your voice is finally heard, you'll have the chops to back it up.

A band is as much about banter as it is ballads.

Ever go to a concert of a band you've followed and loved on radio/streaming forever and were bored to stone seeing them live? I blame the studio (social media translation: content studio). With access to every technological marvel known to recording (including the rightfully maligned AutoTune), a decent engineer can make just about anybody sound good. But only practice and constant performance can turn a studio player into a live performance master.

I once saw the late, great B.B. King perform. He was incredibly overweight, barely made it to his chair onstage, and looked like he was going to play a few hits, collect his check and go. And then he, and his incredible band, began to play. The guy was a god onstage—and a big part of his show involved banter.

What's banter? It's the between song talking that allowed Mr. King to tell jokes, provide context about the next song, rip (good-naturedly) on his band, and best of all, let us get to know him on a first-name basis. No one left that concert without thinking they'd made a friend for life.

And here's the thing: he didn't play as well as he used to, he didn't sing as well either. And no one cared one little bit. He was 100% himself, and that's all that mattered.

Social media is a party of parties. There's literally something for everyone. And banter? That's the coin of many realms throughout. Need an example? Go to just about any LinkedIn post and page down. The post could be about the most arcane, expert-only topic out there, and it will still generate banter-style conversation, especially if the author of the post actively responds to questions and comments.

By participating in this banter, you are demonstrating that you belong at that party and are actively contributing to its success. *You know, that's exactly how you get invited to any party, right?*

Managing a band with the power of naïveté.

Like any male in his early twenties, I joined a rock band for one reason: To make great music, of course!

The year was 1999, and I was 22 and just finished school. My buddy from college asked, "Do you want to join a band?" I said, "Yeah, for sure!" He said, "Ok good. The only thing that's available is drums."

There was only one problem. I didn't know how play drums. In fact, I didn't play any instrument at all. How hard could it be?

Pretend you're playing basketball, and you dribble toward the basket to shoot a layup. If you shoot with your right hand, you jump off of your left foot, right? Drumming is like shooting a layup with your right hand, and jumping off of your right foot.

That when things get a little weird. When you try drumming, there's a lot of stumbling at first, but eventually, you "unlearn" your coordination. After a short period of time you develop something called four-way independence, where all your limbs start doing things independently of one another. It's very cool. (Just so you know, I can tap my head and rub my stomach like a champ.)

Notice I didn't say anything about actually knowing how to read or write music? I've written dozens of songs and performed hundreds of times as a drummer, yet never learned that skill.

Of the four members in our band, I was deemed the 'most businesslike,' so I ended up doing all of our management and booking.

As a manager of a band, you're tasked with stuff like this:

1. Finding a practice space

2. Ensuring that everyone in your band actually shows up to practice (surprisingly hard for most bands)

3. Creating an environment conducive to writing music

It was my job to find the place where we could have a creative outlet. A place where we could write those awesome songs we know we had inside of us. A place with which we could associate creating OUR art.

Are you creating YOUR art?

Do you have that place with which YOU have a positive association, to help put you in your creative mode? If not, find one. It makes all the difference.

Lesson #1
Embrace–and leverage–your naiveté

Be naive. We didn't know if we we're good, and in fact, it's probably best everyone in our band grew up playing sports instead of music. We didn't talk ourselves out of success before we achieved it. Create YOUR art and put it out to the world. You have no right to determine how talented you are. Let the marketplace decide that.

When you have a degree of success with a band, you need a proper band manager. It's mainly because you start having really hard conversations. Contract prices, the kind of Gatorade in the green room…that sort of thing.

So, we hired a band manager. His name was James T. Potat. Jimmy was overqualified by every measure. He had his law degree, he played in a whole series of bands in Britain, and he was unequivocally, without a doubt, completely made up by me. Yes, you read that right, Mr. Potat is the name of my band managing alter-ego. Crazy, but it worked.

Lesson #2
Every band needs a 'bad cop.'

When you need to have hard conversations, hire someone to do that for you. If you can't afford it, just make somebody up and blame him instead. It works really well! My next business idea— BlameSomebodyElse.com. Steal if you want.

Like any kid growing up Milwaukee, I dreamed of being a rock star at Summerfest. It's officially the World's Largest Music Festival and with 700 bands over 11 days on 11 stages, it's an incredible event. If our band could play at Summerfest, that would be incredible validation.

We started pursuing that goal the wrong way, though. We tried to book our own gigs. Instead of going to venues that already had bands and asking them, "Can we play here?" we created our own shows. They looked great from a sound & light standpoint, but the audience wasn't quite the size we hoped.

I remedied this by accident. I started checking out band posters and saw a little icon in the bottom corner with somebody's name on it. I said, "Who is that person?" The bands advertised on the posters were really huge, and they had opening acts performing with them. I figured he'd know something about that.

I called the guy on the poster and asked, "What do you do?" He replied, "I'm a band promoter."

I said, "May I ask your advice? How can we be those bands that open for those bigger bands than us? How can we perform in front of the crowds they draw?"

He said, "I'll show you." And he did. And we followed his advice.

Fast forward to February 2002. The crowd we were performing for in Lafayette, Indiana numbered 1,100, and we continued to play many shows just like that one.

Then, when yours truly contacted Summerfest, he said, "Look at all these great shows that we played...all these great venues. We've been vetted by people that aren't you, so you can feel good about booking us now, right?

The people from Summerfest said, "of course you can play here."

Lesson #3
Go where your audience already is.

You don't need to create your own scene. Create YOUR art. Go where a need already exists, and make yourself valuable. Ask yourself "Where can I go right now and 'perform' for a crowd that already needs what you offer?" The answer to that question is your first solid step toward the success you seek.

It's not all about you (even though it is).

For many people, promoting someone else is far easier than doing it for yourself. If you're not currently engaged in social media because for that very reason, create your own James T. Potat, and put his promotion playbook into practice.

Here's great way to start.

1. Find a practice space.

There's a lot of ROTOMA work you can do anywhere, and on the fly (typically via low-friction channels like Twitter and Instagram), but you really do need a designated place where you can practice your craft uninterrupted. Where do you do focused work best? Start there.

2. Ensure that everyone in your band actually shows up.

In this case, the band is you. And you have to show up, ideally, every day. You'll be surprised, just like budding musicians, just how quickly 15 minutes of focused practice can build your chops—and how 15 minutes of focused practice turns into 30, 45, ...

3. Create an environment conducive to writing music.

Dedicate just one hour a day in a conducive atmosphere, and soon, you'll be performing like a pro (see *Personal Branding Power Hour*, page 155). It could be at home, at work before or after hours, or wherever/wherever works best for you. Pro ROTOMA Tip: A lot of those folks in coffee shops with open laptops? Social media band practice.

Sharing, not shilling.

True story: a client of mine is finally waking up to the potential of social media. Hallelujah for that. The problem is, they are rock solid certain that the best way to use it (for them) is as an always-on megaphone for their products and services. The online equivalent of dragging their catalog behind an airplane over a baseball game.

They don't 'get it,' like a health club that creates a smoking station right outside their front door. But you know clients—they're always right.

Except when they are not.
And this is one of those critical exceptions.

Describing it in the simplest way possible, social media is for sharing, not shilling. It's predicated on the cliché that launched a million bumper stickers: Love. The more you give, the more you'll receive.

An important thing to note: the word is love. Not respect, customer service, or value. The latter are marketing blah blah buzz words of little to no real common meaning anymore. But love? That's existential, elemental, and universally understood.

The real marketing key to social media success (and the 'killer app' reason for doing it) is all about building relationships through a variety of no-cost, always-on channels that enable almost friction-less, real time action.

Social media channels provide the engage now venue for reciprocal conversation, message amplification, and instant notification. Need examples: quick tip videos of FAQs, fast answering mini-help desks, and 'you asked for it, you got it' user-generated content uploaded via their always-in-hand mobile printing presses/movie studios/photo agencies devices.

Premier Guitar gets it—big time.

You don't have to be a guitar player to appreciate just how well the magazine *Premier Guitar* shares socially. Their ROTOMA quotient is amazing. If you're a subscriber to their feed on any of the channels they religiously operate, you're treated to a near-daily barrage of highly valuable, and personally valued, sharing. Here's a look at just some of the quality content they so freely deliver to their fans.

Facebook

Got a few minutes for lunch? Join *PG* guitar ace John Bohlinger as he Facebook Lives *Lunch with Bohlinger* featuring the coolest new & old gear (in this case a '54 Les Paul).

Instagram

Want a little guitar and gear-flavored aperitif all day long? *PG*'s got you covered.

YouTube

PG's Rig Rundown series is simply fantastic. Ever wonder what your personal guitar hero is using to get his/her signature tone? Get the answer, in person, on video.

As of this writing, they've got 322 of them, including Peter Frampton, Angus Young, Esmé Patterson, and one of my favorites, Jason Isbell. It's literally a webseries of guitar geeks geeking out about their guitars—and 100% YouTube FREE. And it's all 100% evergreen content with a perennial ROI that needs to be recalculated daily.

One Rig Rundown episode featuring John Mayer's gear has been viewed (as of this writing) over 1.3+ million times since its posting in 2010—and it's still in their Top Ten playlist.

Not bad for a YouTube-quality video filmed during a pre-concert sound check. And the guitarist cred coolest thing about it? Mayer's not even in it (but the late great Stevie Ray Vaughan's guitar tech Rene Martinez is).

Hear all about John Mayer's concert rig
from the late, great Stevie Ray Vaughan's guitar tech?
That's quality content regardless of the production values.

That means those 1.3+ million views aren't from non-player JM fans; they are from 'how does he get that tone' guitar players who'd rather buy gear than golf. And that's exactly the audience every music-gear Marketing Director wants.

Website

And their magazine? IT'S FREE TOO (online). Go to *Premier Guitar* online and look to the top navigation bar, all the way to the right over the search box.

But wait—there's more.

On top of their Rig Rundown web-video series, they have a DIY repair/modification series, a playlist called Monsters of High Gain, and the list goes on. The screenshot below provides just a taste of the video content guitar-oriented goodness *PG* shares out into the world—again, for FREE. Make no mistake: none of these videos are high-cost productions. But the ROI on what little they do spend is MASSIVE.

*What's all this content sharing
do for Premier Guitar?*

**It gets them the inventory to sell to their customers.
Their real customers: music industry brands.**

That's right. They print a magazine IRL, but their subscribers aren't *PG's* primary buyers. *PG* knows what their real product is: the time, eyeballs, and wallets of rabid toneseekers and those afflicted with really bad G.A.S. (Guitar Acquisition Syndrome).

Premier Guitar is MADE OF PEOPLE!!!

I hate to think of myself and my guitar-wielding cohort as inventory, but that's exactly what we are. That FREE online issue? Count the number of ads in any issue and then compare it to the mass of editorial content. Truth be told, each issue is more of a product catalog for the biggest names in musical instruments.

And guess what; I don't care one little bit. In fact, I am absolutely delighted to help *Premier Guitar* in any way I possibly can because they earned it via the high quality, deeply desirable content they so freely share.

Good sharing begets goodwill— and ultimately, great customers.

The best salesmen have known this forever; Creating and maintaining a great relationship is more important than shilling a great product. A ten-year relationship will always beat a one-time transaction. 'Top of Mind Awareness' has always been fundamental to building and nurturing this kind of relationship. And right now, social sharing is the key that opens the door to real, sustainable, mutually beneficial two-way relationships.

That's why when it comes to social media and making sure my ROTOMA is as good as it can possibly be, my #1 recommendation is **Share. Don't shill**.

The one social media strategy that works everywhere.

One day, while booking shows for Myopic Son, something hit me like a lightning bolt. I realized that success as a rock band—just like everything else—was more about networking than talent. That was a depressing realization for me, the musician. But me the natural-born promoter? I knew exactly what I had to do.

Band promoters are the ones who have the power to get you exposure, especially to groups that you're not already in front of, so you need to get networked with band promoters.

Myopic Son radio interview circa 2002

Way back in 2002 I dialed, that's right actually dialed a hard-lined phone, the number for a local band promoter that I found on one of his flyers around town. He operated under the pseudonym Joe Miller.

He said, "I don't know you, but I get calls like this a lot. If you help me out on my street team, I'll take another look at your band. You can volunteer to stand outside venues and hand out flyers and demo CDs of other bands before my shows."

I was more than willing to serve on Joe's street team, but with so many other bands calling him, he already had a volunteer waitlist that was several months long.

So I asked him what else he needed.

"I guess I need a website," Joe said.

Joe was in the business of selling tickets directly to consumers. He didn't like losing a cut of his profits to Ticketmaster, so he wanted a website that would help him sell more tickets. He also wanted to include a button that would allow visitors to play the most famous song from a band in case they didn't recognize the band name.

I posed to Joe, "Ok, so you want to play a song on your website. What's your budget?"

"What do you mean?" He asked. "I thought this was quid pro quo."

"No Joe, I'm not going to charge you," I said. "But what's your bandwidth budget? You're going to have to send a song file ALL the way across the internet. That costs money."

Remember, this was 2002, long before YouTube, Spotify, or Shazam.

To build this website, Joe was going to need a lot of bandwidth. In order to include bands' music on his website, Joe would have to pay a fee every time a visitor played a song.

Now that exchange may sound comical today, but at the time, it was the only option. And because of that, Joe opted in immediately, without a second's hesitation. He was an early pioneer in digital marketing, and he wasn't hamstrung by choosing between investing in eight different social media platforms.

The difference between 'band' and 'brand'?
R (you ready).

1. When you have too many options, it's easy to get apathetic and never pull the trigger. When there's only one option, you are free from the paralysis of choice.

2. The best way to get your own story out there is to help tell other people's stories. By building Joe a marketing website, we were helping him tell the exact story he wanted to tell ('I bring bands to town that you love'). In turn, Joe helped my band get into the venues and perform for the audiences we wanted.

It would be much easier, and much cheaper, to build Joe's website today using links to YouTube or Spotify. But with so many options available, building his digital media strategy would be harder, not easier.

I speak regularly to groups of marketing executives about social media strategy. The number one request I get ahead of these speaking engagements is to enlighten the group about the emerging platforms. They ask me, "What's the next platform that I don't even know about yet?"

But here's the problem. They haven't even mastered the platforms that are already available, so why should they immediately try to jump onto the next one? They're struggling with the stress of opportunity. They won't commit to any one strategy on any one platform because they second guess their decisions.

How do you get past this paralysis? Simple. Pick one strategy that works across all platforms, and then pick the platforms that make sense based on the demographics of your customers.

OK, but what's one strategy that will work on any platform? Remember my experience with my band?

The best way to get your own story out there is to help tell other people's stories.

You don't want to be the guy in the band wearing his own band's T-shirt. Everyone in the audience already knows the band you're in. That's why they're at your show. Use your time on stage to help highlight someone else's band.

It's not always about what you say. It's more about how you react to what other people say. Take every opportunity you can to promote other people in a way that provides context and meaning to your audience. This is not the same thing as just offering meaningless "shoutouts" to other brands or leaders in your industry. Introduce your audience to the people, organizations, and ideas that they need to know about or that could solve their problems.

New technology or new platforms should never change your strategy.

Use your voice and your influence to provide PR for other people. Fit your message to the platform and you will gain gratitude and respect from your audience. That's the only social media strategy you'll ever need.

ROTOMA / WHAT & WHERE

Talk to enough socially phobic folks and you'll discover a pattern. Most know they should participate, but the sheer number of possible channels, and the speed at which they are irrelevant, stops them cold. How can you reap the benefits of social media top of mind awareness without losing sanity, life balance, or worst of all, job? **Read on.**

A picture worth a thousand fears.

I'm not afraid to say it: Social media is scary. And one brilliant picture sums up the mind-killing fear it engenders perfectly.

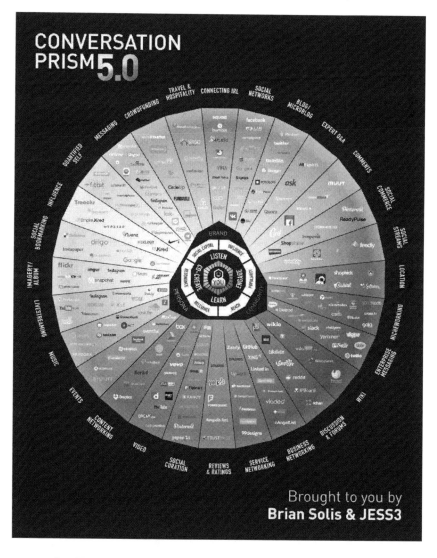

It's like a movie poster for a horror film. Be afraid. Be very afraid.

This incredibly elegant infographic, created by the expert team of JESS3 and Brian Solis, is in its 5.0 version. And guess what, in the true spirit of social media, it's available to you for FREE download, reference and use at conversationprism.com. Go there and get it right now. Don't worry, I'll wait.

OK, we're back. Now blow that sucker up as big as you possibly can on your computer screen. Stare at the the very center of this prism, give into the primal despair that lives there, let it wash over you, and say this along with me.

"I recognize that I will NEVER, EVER be able to fill all of these channels with rich, meaningful content. BUT THAT WILL NOT STOP ME FROM TRYING! GET THEE BEHIND ME EVIL NEO-PENTAGRAM OF SOCIAL DESPAIR! I will do what I can, where I can, wherever I can! You hold no power over me anymore, Dread Lord of Social Media Logos!"

There now. Feel any better? The first step toward a successful, scalable, and sustainable ROTOMA strategy is to admit and accept that at the macro-level, you are powerless. But at the micro? You can do it.

What's here today may be gone tomorrow, but social media is forever.

Many of the ideas and arguments in this book center around this graphic representation of social media *as it stands today*. Keep in mind that this is the fifth iteration of the Conversation Prism that Brian Solis and JESS3 have created.

If I had a request for those two master social media magicians, I would sure like to see an interactive overlay version of the prism that enables us to compare and contrast versions 1.0 to 5.0. My guess? There are far more logos that have been voted off the island from 1.0 than remain on it in 5.0.

That's a critical point of this book too. Much has been made in the corporate world about buggy whip manufacturers that went out of business with the advent and popularity of automobiles. Well, that's true of social media too.

Devoting your focus solely on one social channel is the proverbial one egg in one basket. Diversification is a must—just make sure you're not too diversified. Dilution is just as bad. To do three things well and often is always more important than doing 30 things poorly and inconsistently.

You'll notice that this book is broken up into a variety of brief sections (to call them chapters is an over-statement). That's by design. Spencer and I wanted you to be able to dip in and out of this book at will, always getting something meaningful and actionable that you could use right away. This is more of a manual than a book, and more of a "You can do it!" than a series of "How Tos."

Don't let that stop you from an A to Z read if that's what you're into. I think there's a lot to be gained from the way we ping pong back and forth, riffing off each others takes.

That's exactly what social media is and does. A question or comment is posted, a conversation starts, and sometimes, a revolution begins.

ROTOMA wants YOU!

We invite you to enlist in the truly revolutionary army that is defining this terrifying, and terrific, area of human endeavor. The benefits (and joys) are many, but just like anything worth doing, it's not always easy. With social media, you're never alone—assuming you enlisted. Now get out there and give me 50 (tweets)!

Personal Branding Phobia: it's time to get over it.

During my social media training sessions, I like to spend a little bit of time talking about personal branding. "What does personal branding mean to you?" I ask my audience.

"Anyone?"

Crickets.

That's when they start to squirm. For many people, especially those working in legal, banking, and other professional service industries, the idea of personal branding makes them uncomfortable. "That's just not my thing," they'll say, although they can't always put a finger on why.

After having these conversations with hundreds of professionals around the country, I've narrowed it down to three irrational fears that keep people from embracing personal branding.

1. It feels like cheating on my firm/company.

My audiences often divide down the middle on the question of whether personal branding should be done on company time or personal time. For those who vote personal time, they are convinced that personal branding is primarily about advancing their own career independently of their company.

Here's why I disagree. Think about LeBron James. As a professional athlete, James's personal brand grew significantly during his time playing for the Miami Heat, compared with the beginning of his career with the Cleveland Cavaliers.

Personal brand *vs.* Company brand?
No, Personal brand + Company brand = >!

The Heat's success during his tenure there—winning two national championships—and the affluent, aspirational setting of sunny South Beach, Florida made LeBron James a household name in a way that he had never been in Cleveland.

When he returned to Cleveland, do you think the Miami Heat regretted the fact that he had played for them at all? No. The Heat will forever be associated with back-to-back-championships under the leadership of MVP Lebron James, no matter what team he plays for.

It's the same with any law firm, bank, financial services firm, or any other profession. Your employer will reap the benefits of every second you spend building your personal brand.

2. I'm not LeBron James.
What am I supposed to share?

Everybody thinks they have to be somebody before they can begin their personal branding campaign. They think, "I have to be famous in order to have credibility. Why would anyone pay attention to anything I say?" Well, guess what—you don't need to be LeBron, or have anywhere near his level of fame, for that matter.

Your credibility comes from your experience. If you write about what you've done, why you did it, and how it worked for you, no one will ever question your credibility.

Sometimes it takes brainstorming with another person to realize what it is you do automatically, or what you've figured out without realizing it, that is worth sharing. Everyone has something.

Everyone has a set of best practices they have developed that make them an expert at their job. It could be as simple as a developing an end-of-the-day checklist that you follow to set yourself up for success the next day.

That's what defines what we call content marketing. It's saying, "I figured this out, and I thought you might be able to learn from my mistakes."

When it comes to sharing best practices, some people are afraid of giving away the store. *"If I share all my secrets, why will people pay for my services?"* The answer: the credibility you will gain by sharing your expertise will more than make up for any DIY-oriented clients you will lose by demonstrating exactly how you excel at doing your job.

3. OK, what if I do get famous? Won't I look like an egomaniac?

I have noticed that people have a real fear of success when it comes to personal branding. "Isn't it just going to sound like I'm bragging? When I share stuff about me, won't it sound like, 'Look at me! I'm on the cover of *Time* magazine!'"

I get it. I get the sensitivity to being braggadocious. Everyone has that one person in their social media newsfeed who has poisoned the well for them about personal branding. They post all the time about the size of their network, or they humble-brag, fish for compliments, or worst of all, beg for likes "and I'll like you back." Nobody likes, hires, dates, or marries the desperate.

Let me reassure you on this: If you're afraid of becoming that person, you're already safe, because you're self-aware. The people who abuse personal branding don't have the self-awareness to see that they're not providing any value.

If you approach personal branding from the perspective of a servant leader, your posts will always be honorable. Think about Jim Collins' characteristics of a Level 5 Leader from *Good to Great*: When things go well, the Level 5 Leader gives credit to her team. But when things go south, the buck stops with her. She looks in the mirror and says it's my fault.

Build your brand by highlighting the people around you who are doing great work, sharing the lessons you have learned from your experiences, and admitting your own mistakes.

For 9 out of 10 people, if you ask them who they are, but tell them they can't talk about their profession, they'll be lost for words. As people, we identify so strongly with our professions that we can't help but live and breathe our jobs.

Why not capitalize on that tendency and take it one step further? Build your brand on the back of your experiences at your employer, shining a spotlight on the company and the people who have given you a platform to excel.

What do pork bellies and professional services have in common? They're commodities.

In the professional services world, dozens of businesses make the same lazy marketing mistake: **They use commoditized statements to advertise their brand.**

- "We have the best customer service."

- "We offer the best value for the price"

- "We really care."

The marketing teams at these companies are so entrenched in the business that they forget to step back and evaluate these statements as an outsider. Perhaps you truly have the best customer service, but saying you do does not prove anything.

If anybody can also say it about *their* business, it's a commoditized statement, and it does nothing to differentiate your brand.

Most professional service businesses—banks, law firms, accounting firms, etc.—offer essentially the same services. So how can these companies differentiate themselves? By shining a spotlight on the people who work there.

To differentiate yourself, you have to identify what is unique about your business. And the only thing that is truly unique about your business is the people who work there.

And that's the most important aspect of personal branding; it enables service businesses to differentiate themselves from all of their competitors.

How do you do personal branding at a corporate level?

The first step is to empower your employees to tell their own stories on social media, especially LinkedIn. Any time they invest in building their personal brand while working for your company is time spent building the company's brand.

The next step is to use your corporate platform to tell your employees' stories. Why do they do what they do? What makes them proud? Why do they feel that their work at your company is critically important?

In my work providing social media marketing strategy for law firms, banks, and financial services organizations, I've seen many examples of companies that embraced personal branding and leveraged it to grow their business, as well as companies that have missed great opportunities because they weren't ready to try something new.

Here are two examples of how to apply personal branding strategies to a business:

Leverage the 'feel good' power of anniversaries.

Most companies build some kind of publicity campaign around their big anniversaries—25 years, 50 years, 100 years, etc. Surviving in business for multiple decades lends credibility to a brand and is absolutely worth celebrating.

However, these anniversaries also give you permission to do something that very few companies are.

Drawing on the principles of personal branding—shining a spotlight on the people who make your organization unique—here are two ways you could approach celebrating that anniversary:

• Invite your employees to share their own significant milestones that they will celebrate that year: 20th wedding anniversary, 30th high school reunion, finally becoming debt free.

• Invite your clients who are celebrating a significant anniversary to share their stories on your social media and blogging platforms. What lessons has a small tool and die shop learned from 45 years in business? How much has the printing industry changed in 30 years and how has a local printer adapted? How has a local construction company survived to the third generation?

And let's be clear, the point of these campaigns is NOT to go to your clients or employees fishing for compliments. You're not trying to end each anniversary story with a quote such as, "And there's no way we would have survived as long as we have without an amazing relationship with our banker/lawyer/advisor!" You're not trying to position yourself as the savior. But by making your clients or your employees look good, you look good. That's all you have to do.

A big award is big news.

When businesses win impressive awards from industry associations or publications—like *Fortune* magazine's '100 Best Companies to Work For,' or a local business publication's 'Business of the Year' award, or a construction trades association's Contractor of the Year award, etc.—they often throw a big party, print a few banners and plaques to display around the office, and then call it a day.

They're missing a big opportunity. An award like this creates an opportunity to provide enormous value to your current and potential clients too.

Share how you did it.

Business awards usually require a complicated application process that may involve surveying your employees or your clients and assembling materials to submit to a panel of judges. If you have won an award multiple times, you may have developed some time-saving tricks and learned some lessons about the best ways to guarantee consistent performance.

The expertise that you have gained is knowledge that your clients could benefit from, even though it may seem completely unrelated to your core business function. An insurance company or a law firm will gain credibility in the eyes of its clients and potential clients by sharing its own case study of how to win a prestigious award.

In the example of an award recognizing you as a top place to work, you can take that opportunity to put whoever is responsible for maintaining your company culture, which is probably not the CEO, in the spotlight.

Share the impact the award is having on your company.

If the awards you win are truly meaningful (and thus worth promoting), they will have a lasting impact on your company. Perhaps the awards serve as motivation to your teams to work harder all year long, and winning the award gives them pride in what they do. Or perhaps the award reflects the culture that you have created by treating your employees as well as you do your clients.

When you share how you won the award, you should share the impact it has had on your employees. The implicit message is "Now that we won this award, we want to show you how you could win it too and why you should want to."

An award gives you an opportunity to speak from authority. Don't miss that opportunity.

Personal branding can guide your corporate marketing strategy and help you differentiate yourself by providing real value to your clients. Start both embracing and implementing these ideas **now**.

Think you're 100% unique?
You're 100% right, and 100% wrong.

In youth, there's a tendency to think you are an absolutely unique being. That no one could possibly feel or think the same as you do. And as a youth, you were absolutely right.

Then as you grow up, if you're paying attention, you'll start to see patterns of behavior and preference coalescing all around you all the time. Like when did kale become a thing? You spend a lifetime gloriously ignorant of this green, leafy vegetable, then suddenly, everyone's got a taste for it. Are we all just creatures of habit and herd? Why yes, we are.

In truth, human beings are both. Lone poets in a tower, and herd animals waiting for the next stampede.

Knowing that, how can you possibly stand out?
By standing up on social media.

You have a voice that deserves to be heard, and blended into the universal context we all share. You are distinct, yet not alone. And if you're any good at what you do, there's an audience waiting to hear from you.

The secret to achieving Expert status online? Act, post, and respond like one–and repeat x 1000.

It doesn't happen overnight, and is directly correlated to the energy and hustle you devote to it, but the coveted title 'Expert' is achievable by anyone who wants it—assuming the following criteria:

1. Demonstrable mastery within your niche;

2. Laser-focus on relevance within your defined niche;

3. Open sharing of relevant, and audience-valued properties (e.g., ideas, advice, mentorship, downloadable content).

Find your social media spirit animal.

I am a constant follower of Melanie Deziel on Twitter, et al. She's effortlessly living the 'got everything' lifestyle so many crave, wearing a chic black & white wardrobe while jetting to exotic locations to serve up her wisdom re: native advertising to ravenous locals.

Or so I thought. Then I listened to Grant Baldwin's *The Speaker Lab* podcast, episode #51, where she pulled the curtain back to reveal how she got that ab-fabulous life. And it all came down to just a few simple (but hard) things:

- Strategic vision
- Hustle
- Relevance
- Hustle
- Research
- Hustle
- Discipline
- Hustle

And then, only AFTER all that:
- Luck

Melanie may not know it (but surely suspects by now) that I have selected her to be my social media spirit animal—or, to be more exact—my rabbit. Every performance-oriented greyhound needs one. And I'm basing my personal/professional social media strategy on her relentless example. She's like of a less caffeinated Gary Vaynerchuk—and with a far better wardrobe.

Melanie's living La Vida Work Your Hind Off,
and her ROTOMA proves it.

Like a snowball at the top of a hill, the ROTOMA from Melanie's consistent effort is cumulative. She's now on the top tier of speakers within her field globally. She keeps her snowball rolling at a pretty fast tempo, and her results reflect that.

That tempo, quality of work, relevancy of content, and open sharing has allowed her to leave a job at *The New York Times* (one fantastic gig) to pursue her own passion projects like speaking on native advertising and content marketing all over the world (an even better gig—that she owns. *Remember, if you don't own in, it's not yours*).

ROTOMA to your own drummer.

Here's the thing; Melanie's tempo may not be for you. It certainly isn't for me. But that doesn't mean I can't follow her lead at a tempo that's more amendable to my lifestyle and ambition. And that's the thing about tempo. Like a metronome, you can adjust it to your current 'best' performance level, then crank it up as that level improves. What may have to be a comfortable *andante* today can easily ramp up to *allegro* whenever you're ready to rock.

Here's another musical metaphor that makes the point: There are far more campfire strummers than speed metal guitar gods. But that should never stop you from picking up a guitar and starting to play. The more you play, the better you get—and the larger your audience grows.

ROTOMA is a song anyone can, and should, play.

There are just too many professional and personal benefits not to. All it takes is the desire, and the willingness to practice, and the ability to deal with not being perfect right out the gate.

And by the way, that kind of vulnerability actually endears you to your audience. But don't take my word for it. Check out Brené Brown's TED Talk on Vulnerability. There's a reason it's got > 30MM views. www.ted.com/talks/brene_brown_on_vulnerability

So what's your instrument and expertise? Get out there, share your voice and viewpoint loud and proud, and watch your audience discover you.

Know your REAL product.

My very first Creative Director once said to me one of those supposedly insightful but at the time mildly mystifying marketing truisms:

"People don't go out to buy drills.
They go out to get holes."

After mentally flipping him off and mumbling 'Thanks, Yoda,' I began to chew on that pithy insight. And have been masticating that cud ever since. It's like the saying 'have your cake and eat it too,' and just as annoying > provocative > and ultimately profound.

To me, 'buy holes' has become shorthand that means it doesn't matter what you're selling; your product is really whatever the customer actually wants. Not your product, but the outcome of the customer's interaction with that product.

Here's what I mean. Brazil's CNA ostensibly sells language lessons. But that's not their real product. This is: real, human connection.

And to be specific in this case: a real, human connection between Brazilian kids who want to learn English, and senior citizens in America who want to help.

To experience how powerful this product is, head to YouTube and watch the video (search 'CNA speaking exchange').

CNA - Speaking Exchange / YouTube

For CNA, learning a foreign language is truly about one thing: human connection. And this video manifestation of this understanding is just so elegantly smart and socially sharable. As of this writing, this video has received over 1.67 MM views. Not bad for a company selling a commodity (foreign language classes). But their version is no commodity. It's pure premium branded, emotionally potent, and got ROTOMA written all over it.

Not drills. Holes.

CNA and their brilliant agency FCB Brazil understand this simple truth, and created a program that enabled wonderful new connections between South American teens and North American seniors. In sharing that story in such an open, 'not even soft sell' way, they created a virally potent video they can and do legitimately share as part of a master ROTOMA strategy. **Good content begets social sharing, and social sharing begets 'top of mind' relevance and remembrance.**

Most people & businesses focus on features.
But friends & customers *buy* solely on benefits.

Understanding that one idea is probably the most important thing for marketers to understand. You sell features. **But they buy benefits.** I recommend you tattoo the latter phrase on the back of both of your hands—and always heed those words whenever talking to someone who actually uses your products or services.

Translating that to the personal realm, consider the typical LinkedIn profile. It's like the back of a personal sales sheet. Nothing but features (specifications). I went to school there; worked here, here, and here; and received these honors, accreditations and awards. Oh, and some marketing buzz word salad about leveraging this, engaging that, and optimizing for...FEATURES.

That's fine for the HR bots that scrape the site, searching for a set of carefully defined keywords. But ROTOMA should never be a keyword driven exercise in SEO blah biddity blah. It should show you at your finest, *demonstrating* your savvy, experience, and value, not just touting the features of your past.

**One of the central tenets of ROTOMA is 'Show, don't Tell'.
But the next, critical question is: What are you showing?
The answer: your REAL product.**

What's your REAL product?

The very top sales professionals have known this forever: *I am not the products I sell—I am the product itself.*

A truly great sales pro can sell anything—because their REAL product is their unique combination of diligence, discipline, charm, personality, follow-through, and ability to learn, present, and promote any product feature set.

In social media, you are the product. So stripping away all the features, what is your REAL product persona?

You are a 'type'. But which 'type?'

Matchmaker, Promoter, Thinker, Curator, Creator, Amplifier, Fixer, Tastemaker—these are all types of social media 'REAL personas.' The perfect ROTOMA strategy would have you wearing all of these hats at one point or another, but the reality is, in your default state you're just one. But how do you know which one is really you?

Look at the posting style that accounts for the majority of your social media activity.

Are you writing 1,000+ word blog posts on a weekly basis (with a sprinkling of 'hey, this is cool, and you should be paying attention to it' curation posts)? You're a **Thinker**.

Are your feeds full of *Unselfish Selfies* (see page 189) that are full of @ signs identifying the people you met, where you met? You're a **Promoter**.

Are you constantly introducing people via whatever social channel makes sense? You're a **Matchmaker**.

Like a baseball player on a high performing team, ROTOMA wants you to be able to play every position on the field when necessary. But it also demands that you focus on your primary specialty. A pitcher can be a catcher in a pinch, but a pitcher's first focus is striking out batters by throwing heat. So what's your heat?

Spencer is a fantastic Promoter because he's a natural at it, going all the way back to his Myopic Son days. That doesn't mean he's not also a Thinker, Matchmaker, Amplifier, etc. But his personal sweet spot, IMHO, is in promoting (enthusiasm, people, the concept of ROTOMA, the work of others….).

Me? I guess I default to a Thinker point-of-view. While I can whip out the occasional *bon mot* with the best of them, I keep them (for the most part) to myself online to avoid the inevitable flame wars and 'what I meant to say' misunderstandings. But deeper dives, yeah, those feel good to me—but not too deep. Keep the topic tight, go easy on the word count, make the point, and move on. And so I do—and am.

What is your REAL product? What's your default, but perfectly authentic, online persona? Answer one of those questions, and you've probably answered both.

Now get out there and be the true 'who' you are.

ROTOMA–the ROI of Social Media Top of Mind

LinkedIn means business.

Big data. Business intelligence. Predictive analytics. Strategies reserved for huge companies with huge budgets, right? Wrong.

Have a LinkedIn profile? Then I'm talking to you.

In 2016, Microsoft turned heads in the tech and social media world when it bought LinkedIn for $26 billion. That's 26,000 *million* dollars.

As a company that had never dabbled in social media, Microsoft's decision seemed like an odd choice to many. But to me, it made perfect sense. **Microsoft was investing in the biggest treasure trove of business intelligence in the world**. And that store is only growing bigger—LinkedIn reached a milestone 500 million members in April of 2017, and it continues to gain more and more users every single day, each of whom is bringing a nearly incalculable amount of business intelligence right along with them.

By owning LinkedIn, Microsoft can now track trends related to employees at large corporations, and trends about employment in general.

Example: If four banking executives from a high-profile bank suddenly update their resumes within a week of each other, it's a good bet that something is changing at that bank. On a basic level, that business intelligence can guide Microsoft as it expands its enterprise-level software operations. But for investors, data points like that are literally priceless. And right now, that kind of invaluable business intelligence is available to you. And the cost to you? $0.00.

Yes, you can get the milk for free.

Luckily, you don't need to spend $26 billion to get access to crucial business intelligence via LinkedIn. **You don't even need to pay for a premium account.**

You can gain valuable insight into the challenges your prospects are facing by simply checking their social media updates.

On LinkedIn, this means navigating to their profile on a regular basis and just observing:

• What are they reading and liking and sharing (you'll find this under Articles & Activity)?

• Have they written any articles?

• What product or service are they advertising on their banner photo?

• Have they changed anything about their work history or their headline (what they do and what they're looking for) recently?

• Are they suddenly updating their profile? How? What areas?

The next step is to navigate to the company page, and repeat the observation process. I have found that most companies use LinkedIn (and other social media platforms) to share the biggest initiatives that they have going on at the moment. That information is critical. After all, you don't want to walk into a meeting not knowing what the company is working on if it was publicly available and actively shared online.

Turning a prospect into a client.
LinkedIn biz intel in action.

I was pitching a banking client and knew I needed to have better business intelligence than my competitors. I had done some basic research on their social media profiles, and I noticed that their profile banners were promoting their mobile app.

I reasoned that they must want more users to download and use the app because it makes them stickier clients who would have a harder time switching banks. I continued to scroll through the feed to see what information they were sharing.

I noticed that they were also making a big deal about the grand opening of a new modern cafe-style bank branch offering popcorn and coffee and inviting customers to hang out.

These two initiatives seemed at odds with each other, so I made a note to ask them about their strategy during my pitch. When I did, I got a response that told me a lot about the company.

They explained that their business model relied on providing great customer service by blending convenience with relationships. The app provides convenience, but the physical interaction through the modern bank branch helps build relationships.

During the rest of our conversation, I was able to focus on how I could come alongside their efforts to provide great customer service in other areas of the business and build on the work they're doing with their app and their branch renovations.

If you're not using LinkedIn to gather business intelligence about your clients (and competitors), then you're missing out on freely available information that could make or break your next pitch.

Why else do you think Microsoft would pay $26 billion for a social network? They want to know who people are at work, and there's no better platform for understanding who someone is at work than LinkedIn.

That's insight you can't afford to live—or work— without.

What's your Flagship?

As a big, geeky fan of the Aubrey/Maturin novels of Patrick O'Brien (you may be familiar with the 2003 Russell Crowe film *Master and Commander: The Far Side of the World* which was based on a couple of O'Brien's books), I can't help but see the social media landscape through the eyes of a naval officer circa 1812.

Without boring you to death, every admiral commands a group of lesser vessels that perform a variety of specialized tasks from the deck of his 'Flagship' headquarters. The Flagship is the hub around which all activity occurs. It develops the strategy and tactics (literally, tactics, as in 'we all turn to starboard NOW'), and issues orders to the rest of the flotilla. Everything originates at the Flagship. And the entire squadron's success depends on it, is configured to protect it, and tasked with extending its power and reach.

So what does an 18th Century naval order of battle got to do with ROTOMA and social media? Everything.

If everything is a priority, nothing is.

I think the biggest reason so many social media lurkers are passive lurkers in the first place is the sheer tonnage of possibilities out there. While I address this 'where to get started' question later in *Step #1: One Step* (see page 141), I think it's imperative to introduce this key concept first: **pick a Flagship social media channel.**

Here's one example that proves the concept.

My good friend Nicole Klein of Charlie & Violet Photography is a fantastic Twin Cities-based photographer specializing in maternity, newborn, and couples photography. Just one of her photos on Instagram is worth somewhere north of a BILLION words.

See what I mean? Her work, talent, and style sells itself—once you've seen it. For her, and many other visually oriented creators, it's a no-brainer: Instagram is her Flagship. She's posting impossible to ignore baby photos on a very regular basis. The fact that Instagram is owned and tightly integrated with Facebook is even better. But for Nicole, social sharing all starts with Instagram. It's her #1 priority—that then feeds everything else.

As a business and brand, she's 100% business-to-consumer (B2C). If she has a LinkedIn presence, I'm completely unaware of it, because I don't need it. She's on Instagram, and that's where I go to find her.

The fast follower channels in her personal social media flotilla are Facebook and her website, and she's cross-posting to all the usual social media suspects, **but her Flagship—the #1 channel for building her brand that's gotten her international attention, followers, and best yet, business—is Instagram*.**

LinkedIn–
The #1 crack in the corporate firewall.

Spencer is all over this elsewhere in the book, but let me underscore a key challenge facing many business people who would like to be top of mind: corporate firewalls.

When it comes to social sharing, highly regulated fields (law, financial services, medical, et al) can have a minefield of compliance and liability issues. But as Spencer points out, LinkedIn is often the one social media site such highly regulated and firewalled businesses allow their associates to use. Its value as a lead generation, brand-building, and ROTOMA-boosting tool is just too strong to be denied.

If you're in tightly regulated sectors like this, look no further. Your Flagship is LinkedIn. Whether you can, or even need to, use other channels for your ROTOMA strategy is highly personal and subject to the specific restrictions you face. Just remember this: entire careers have been built by mastering LinkedIn. If you're 100% business to business oriented (B2B), start there.

Facebook
The right choice for personal touch B2C.

Does the word 'lifestyle' apply to you and your brand? Then Facebook should be your Flagship jam. While there's a ton of commerce happening there every second of every day, it is generally packaged within a softer side 'personality and life enhancement' wrapper.

With the possible exception of the regulated industries discussed above, Facebook is an absolute 'must' for any business, but it's not necessarily the #1 Flagship for you—unless you're pure B2C, and offering highly personalized products and services.

Visual vs. Verbal.
Personal vs. Professional.

Each social media channel has its own, sometimes very subtle, personality characteristics. YouTube vs. Vimeo is very personal vs. professional in style. Same thing with Facebook vs. LinkedIn. That doesn't mean you can't do both—you should do both—but it's essential that you prioritize and choose the 'one ring to rule them all.' If you, like most people, have a limited amount of time for social media activity, it's far better to strategically do fewer things (or channels) better. You don't have to do them all, but the ones you do, you better do well—and often.

Answer these questions to configure
your social media Flagship flotilla.

• Where do you currently originate your social content?

• What channel do you naturally gravitate toward personally?

• Are you primarily visual or verbal?

• If currently active, which channel generates the most engagement with your audience?

• Do you own your Flagship channel*?

Ah, that last question is in **bold** for a reason. Why? Read on, or ignore the rest at your peril....

*If you don't own it, it's not yours.

That last question is one of my 'paranoid in a bunker' bugaboos. I've learned a few too many times the hard way that 'if you don't own it, it's not yours.'

That's why pretty much every single word I've written for social media sharing (including those found in this book) originates from my blog at gettingcre8tive.com. I own my words and URL, and that makes them MINE! I liberally use the © sign too, there and everywhere else I cross-post. I'm more than ok with sharing my toys in the sandbox—but I'm sure everyone knows I'm taking them home with me at the end of the day.

Photographers like Nicole know this pain better than most. Flickr and other sites have muddied the image copyright ownership waters so much that it's forced some visual artists to watermark things to the point of worthlessness. And while she doesn't own Instagram, she owns her copyrights, and her website backs them all up in perpetuity. If Instagram ever pivots, she's hasn't lost a thing. But due to its global reach and audience, Instagram remains her Flagship until that dreaded event takes place (or its supplanted by the 'next big thing').

"But, but…it was always free."

Don't ever think that what's free today won't be tolled tomorrow. Or just gone. Anyone who's ever poured their heart and soul into someone else's site that subsequently shut down or goes pure paid knows the pain of which I write. Don't let it happen to you. Own your Flagship, constantly monitor the state of your social flotilla, and be prepared to tack toward a more amenable harbor when the weather changes (which it always does).

If you're commanding your social destiny from the deck of a strategically sound Flagship, you can sail wherever, whenever. If you haven't already, select your Flagship today, because in the immortal words of Patrick O'Brien's Captain Jack Aubrey, "There is not a moment to be lost."

LinkedIn without the FreakedOut.

For every person who is addicted to social media, there's another person who has sworn it off for fear of getting "sucked into the void." Because of this, there are hundreds of professionals who are missing out on opportunities to use social media outlets, especially LinkedIn, for specific business purposes.

The fear of wasting their effort keeps many people from investing time in engaging with their LinkedIn community. But the fear of just wasting time in general is an equally large obstacle for many people. They recognize that their behavior on Facebook or Pinterest tends to be an addictive response to boredom, and they don't want to give themselves another platform to waste time on.

When they open LinkedIn, they may see a silly inspirational post that has become controversial for no clear reason, and their instinct is to immediately close the page before they get sucked in. I get it. It takes approximately five seconds to get a bad taste for a media outlet. That's how I feel about watching TV most of the time.

But when you write off LinkedIn as "another social media time suck," you miss a huge opportunity to develop new contacts and stay top of mind for your current contacts.

You don't have to participate in the conversations that you don't want to.

Recently, I met a financial advisor at a conference where I spoke in Boston who shared how he does almost all his business development through LinkedIn. He finds potential clients, researches their background and interests, highlights their accomplishments, and then leaves the platform.

LinkedIn is a communication tool that can be used like email to connect with other professionals and grow your network. You don't open your email and scroll through it because you're bored. You open it because you need the communication platform to conduct business. You should approach LinkedIn the same way.

There's a line between using social with a purpose and defaulting to it because you're bored and want to be entertained. The key to using social media for business is to set clear intentions, follow a strategy, and stick to strict time limits.

Here are six tips for making the most of your efforts on social media:

1. Set a time limit and stick to it. I recommend 10 minutes a day, because that should be long enough to do whatever you need, and it will motivate you to skip the news feed altogether. Once you've made the connection you wanted to make, done the research you needed to do, or posted the content you wanted to share, then get off the platform. Don't allow yourself to stay and browse.

2. Focus on your target market. Whether you're in sales, you're searching for a job, or just looking to grow your professional network, you should know who your target market is. You should focus your activity on starting conversations with these targets, whether they're vice presidents at a company you want to earn as a client or they're thought leaders in your industry. Before you log in, make a list of the people you want to engage with.

3. Send personalized connection requests. Stop scrolling and start searching. Find the connection, and send them a connection request with a concise message explaining why you want to connect. And that reason had better not be, "I want to sell you something," or any variation of that phrase. Try out something like this: "I was reading your latest blog post, and I loved your insight on X." Or, "I saw this share on Twitter, and I really liked it."

4. Engage with the content your targets are publishing. Find their posts and their blogs, like, comment, and share them to your network, even if you have to go to another website to find their content. Not everyone embraces LinkedIn's blogging platform yet, so they may share a lot of content elsewhere.

5. Tag people. Before you click "post" on a share of someone else's content or a photo you're uploading, think about whom you can tag in the post.

Tag smart, and you're always 'it.'

Tagging on LinkedIn works like it does on most platforms: Type an @ symbol before the person's name, and LinkedIn will bring up a drop down menu of connections and people you follow to confirm the tag. Click on the correct person, and their name will appear in a blue hyperlink to their profile in your post. The people you tag will receive a notification of the tag and any interaction with your post, and they may even receive an email about the post depending on their LinkedIn profile settings.

But I'll include a serious caveat with this tip: **make sure the posts you tag people in are relevant.** We've all been subject to someone misusing the tagging feature on Facebook to spread awareness about something we have no interest in. On LinkedIn, your tagging should be a way to give someone a heads up that you've said something nice about them and/or their work.

Here's an example: When I was leaving Boston. I noticed that Zoom, the video conferencing platform, had a billboard up in Logan International Airport. I thought it was cool to see a tech company investing in analog marketing, so I snapped a photo and tweeted it, making sure to tag the company. The founder of Zoom then retweeted it, and my post got a high level of engagement.

And finally...

6. Connect with your current customers. Too many people take their current customers for granted. It's not cool or sexy to go after your existing customers and show them love. But reactivating your current customers' loyalty for your brand is equally as important as developing awareness in new targets.

Start by simply connecting with the people you've worked with at all current and former clients. Then find ways to highlight their successes and share content that they will find meaningful.

If you approach LinkedIn with this strategy, you'll be able to reap demonstrable benefits from the time you invest, and you'll avoid wasting time on another news feed.

The 3 Ps–
Ping, Promote, or Proffer.

When thinking about social media, pay special attention to the second word in the phrase: media. The plural form of medium, it lumps every app, website, and service together into one all-encompassing bucket. And for many, that bucket can actually look more like a can of worms: messy, hard to disentangle, and worst case, not worth opening.

In reality, it's not one bucket at all. It can be broken down in any number of ways. By content style (words, video, audio, still photography, etc.), by user experience (purely lean-back passive to richly interactive), and more.

The shelf life of this post would be minutes if I focused solely on currently dominant social channels. But remember, MySpace was once the 800lb gorilla in its space. Things change, and in the social media, they change fast.

Social media is an ever changing, organic universe. Coming up with a list of immutable rules is a fool's errand, because Facebook, Instagram, LinkedIn, and Twitter (the titans of social at the time of this writing) are constantly optimizing, refining, and occasionally pivoting, or completely shuttering their services, regardless of popularity or utility.

My advice: focus on a channel's primary function, not its temporal functionality by boiling them all down to:

The Three Ps: Ping, Promote, or Proffer.

Ping. Promote. Proffer.
The 3 Ps of Social Media Call & Response.

Despite all the hype, the rich intricacy of social media can be broken down to a few primary elements. I submit the following three sharing styles for your consideration and implementation.

PING

A simple, quoted tweet can be the beating pulse of your social media presence. But be careful—too much irrelevant activity might drive followers away.

Ping

aka 'See that blip on your social media radar? That's me!'

Suggested Channel: Twitter (retweets, quoted tweets, status updates, no original content)

Time/Effort Required: Minimal

PROMOTE

aka 'Hey, here's some input I think you'll be interested in.'

Suggested Channels: Twitter (hot takes), Instagram (casual photos), Facebook post, LinkedIn group participation

Time/Effort Required: Some, but nothing too time-consuming.

*Great **Proffer**, Spencer, and nice **Promote**, Barbara.*

Every time you promote someone else, you're actually doing the same for yourself. Contributing your two cents to a LinkedIn post promotes the person who posted it, and enables you to demonstrate your expertise to peers and prospects. It's a win/win for all involved—including your audience.

PROFFER

aka 'My FREE gift of relevant, original content. Enjoy.'

Suggested Channels:
Blog post, YouTube video, downloadable PDF white paper

Time/Effort Required:
As much as you can muster on a regular basis.

'Proffer' is an archaic word with an interesting pedigree but more importantly, it starts with 'P'. Consider it an offering to the Gods of Alliteration.

Making the commitment to be one of social media's 1%, "the Creators,' takes time and discipline, but can be the primary thing that builds your personal brand and identifies you as a valuable 'follow' online and in real life. This post originated at my Getting Cre8tive blog, but is shown here cross-posted at LinkedIn.

Pick a 'P' and get posting.

By categorizing your social media posting via this tri-level system, it's easier to create a doable strategy that doesn't require a dedicated team to implement.

One way to think about this model is as a continuum from least demanding / lightest effort (**Ping**) to most involved / most demanding (**Proffer**). For instance: A 140-character Ping-style tweet requires a far less effort than an original YouTube-based video (**Proffer**).

Ping	Promote	Proffer

Effort Required & Perceived Value

Social Media is a beast that must be fed, but every meal need not be a 1,000-word epic.

A regular posting calendar is a critical component of any social media strategy, but remember creating a calendar is not the same thing as developing content. A calendar is an actionable outline that can make the creation of content if not completely easy, then certainly less painful. How? By showing you graphically that 'it's really not that hard.'

Let's say your strategy calls for you to post something at least twice a week. Two meaningful, well-conceived and -crafted blog posts could require the better part of a day to write, prep and post. Ain't nobody got time for that, assuming social media creation is not your day job. But don't worry; that's the beauty of the 3Ps. If you don't have the time or content to **Proffer**, you can always **Ping** or **Promote**.

A balanced posting week might look something like this:

Monday
Ping *(maybe?)*
Play 'catch up'. **Ping** appropriately (or not at all).
Time/Content creation weight: Light.

Tuesday
Ping
Suggested Channel:
Twitter / could be hot take, retweet, quoted tweet.
Time/Content creation weight: Light.

Wednesday
Promote
Consume social media, **Promote** something you've found.
Time/Content creation weight: Medium.

Thursday
Proffer
(e.g., blog post, cross-posted where possible)
Time/Content creation weight: Heavy.

Friday
Ping
Followups from blog post response
('Like' Likes, shout out to quoted tweets, etc.)
Time/Content creation weight: Medium.

The duration of your efforts might have to be spread out over two-weeks instead of one depending on work, travel, and family obligations. Maybe the specific strategic timing of your social presence should be a little less aggressive. But a schedule, even one this loose, is the skeletal system of strategy and execution is its muscle. Without both working seamlessly together, everything falls apart.

Here's the biggest, baddest secret to this entire 3Ps strategy.

You don't have to be an omniscient social guru. Or a master of video editing, audio production, or any of the industrial-strength tools found in Adobe Creative Suite. And you don't ever have to do any **Proffer** level heavy-lifting to have a successful social media presence on social media. *But you do have to do something* and with clock-like regularly.

Ping on a regular basis.

Promote whomever whenever possible.

And who knows, you just might come up with something worth **Proffering**—and then you can because you've already developed the muscles and skills needed to do so.

Executing the Three Ps (as part of a comprehensive ROTOMA strategy) is like going to the gym. Don't just get the membership. If you want the results, you have to do the work.

So **Ping**, **Promote**, and **Proffer** according to a realistic workout schedule that you can manage and maintain for the long run.

WWWDD?
What would Walt Disney do?

Mickey Mouse is the reason you're not using social media the way you should. Really. And it's all because of Walt Disney. Although Mr. Disney died 50 years before Twitter's launch in 2006, his influence still affects us. But don't worry, I'll show you why and how you can escape Mr. Disney's shadow.

Back when Walt Disney was working with his animators on the original Mickey Mouse cartoons, his animators would show him their proposed sketches before final approval. He'd look at their art and ask, "Can you 'plus' this?" Said another way, "Can you improve on this a little bit?"

They would go back and forth until eventually the animator said, "No, I can't do anything more. Is this good enough?" At that point, Mr. Disney would authorize the sketch. Or not, depending on his mood.

Why all the fuss? Because as each individual cell of an animated filmstrip was hand drawn and painted, and finally approved, it would become part of the feature film. Once the film was approved and duplicated, nothing could be changed. The final version could not be altered or improved upon. And it stayed that way—for time immemorial.

Mr. Disney was fastidious with every detail in those early cartoons, as well as every aspect of his business. His perfectionist mentality still shows in everything the Walt Disney Co. does in its day-to-day business. Any visitor to Disneyland or Disney World can attest to this fact. Each guest interaction with a Disney 'cast member' is choreographed: each experience made as close to *perfect* as possible.

This same unwavering attention to detail permeates modern-day cinema. Computer-generated imagery (CGI) completely blurs the line between what's real and what's not. Film creators, given their enormous budgets and massive manpower, apply perfection in ways Walt Disney could never fathom.

Why does this apply to you? How can Walt Disney and modern-day Hollywood possibly influence your decisions on social media?

One thing I hear when I give speeches or work with clients is, "How do I know if what I'm creating and sharing is 'good enough'?" Fear is the major factor that inhibits our evolution from social media consumer to social media producer. Why? We've grown accustomed to perfection.

When it comes to you and what you share on social media, I want you to think about Mr. Disney and his interactions with his animators. Think about what a perfect social media share would look like and ask yourself, "Can I plus this?"

Also though, and this is critical—add a small caveat. Ask yourself, "If I plus this, will the enhancement make what I share that much better? Is it really going to matter?"

When it comes to creating and sharing on social media, we so often get in our own way. We prevent ourselves from pushing the publish button for one simple reason, and it's because we strive for perfection. In a digital world, everything can be improved upon a tiny bit more. Each element bettered, each individual pixel further enhanced.

Consider your efforts from a very binary standpoint. Say, "If I'm going to invest the extra time to make this social media share as good as I possibly can, is that going to be worth it?"

Once you create that list of options you could do to improve the post, but still feel good OK about NOT doing them, then it becomes much easier to push the publish button.

Use the 'plus it' idea from Walt Disney to decide how and why to create your social media shares. Is striving for perfection holding you back? Assess what you're doing—and not doing—and repeat one mantra to yourself:

80% out the door is better than 100% in the drawer.

Confidently start pushing that publish button more often, and you'll see your content creation start to grow. As a result, the audience whom you serve will value you more and more.

Hot Take or Cold consideration? Both.

Marshall McLuhan, the brilliant media theorist, coined the much misunderstood phrase "The medium is the message." I think he's absolutely right, and wrong, at the same time.

In explaining this concept to others, I point to a traditional advertiser who spends their entire annual marketing budget on a 30-second TV commercial during the game that cannot be named due to overly aggressive copyright enforcement (hint: it starts with 'super', and is part of a compound construction that ends with 'bowl'). An entire year's marketing budget, burned in 30 seconds? What's the point?

The point for that specific advertiser is that ***the medium really is their message***. The fact that they can run with the big dogs, airing a commercial during the most expensive, globally viewed event on earth IS the message. We are mighty, worldwide, and bold. Remember us when you're shopping for _____.

The story I heard back in the day (pre-computerized anything) was that the padlock manufacturer MasterLock did exactly that for years.

They had one very impactful (literally impactful) TV commercial:

A. A padlock hangs from a target.
B. A bullet blows right through the padlock.
C. The MasterLock padlock, shot clean through, stays locked.

They'd run it just once during the "Game That Must Not Be Named," burning through their entire annual marketing budget in 30 seconds—but it didn't matter. They got their message out in a big way. And if you were in the market to buy a padlock, there was only one brand in your mind. The medium was the message—and it worked.

While things have changed significantly, the social medium is still the message stylistically. Let's take a look at just a few of them in action.

Social Media is the message, and comes in a myriad of styles.

I am a little embarrassed to say that this was my very first tweet:

A visionary take? Not so much.

In my defense, this was back in the days of mundane blather like "I wonder what's for lunch today?" updates as everyone tried to make sense of the fledgling medium.

Then a series of world events in 2009 woke up everyone to it's massive potential. The unrest in Moldova, the Green Revolution in Iran, and later, the Ukrainian Maidan Square protests made revolutionary use of Twitter to organize, direct resistance, and overcome censorship of more traditional channels.

Just how powerful can a 140-character message venue be? Ask *former* Ukrainian President Viktor Yanokovych.

Twitter, the natural nest for the Hot Take.

Does the term 'Hot Take' really need a definition? See something, react instantly, whip out your phone, tweet, pic, post. That's how I'd define it. The very idea of 'live tweeting' an event is pure Hot Take.

Careers have been made, and lost, because of this powerful social style. That's why a lot of professionals avoid (and should) such blowback-potential channels, sticking to the safer confines of LinkedIn.

There's a reason LI feels like the lobby of a tony country club—everyone's on their best business behavior all the flippin' time. And when someone transgresses its unspoken rules, the community reacts in a similar way via the subtle shunning technique of 'LinkOuting.'

Hot Take on LinkedIn? High risk, low reward.

So it sounds like one should avoid the Hot Take altogether, right? Not necessarily.

How can you do it in a way to enhance, not hurt, your career and reputation? Check out *Making Conferences Count* (page 183) and *Unselfish Selfies* (page 189).

You can have your Hot Take cake and eat it too, by accentuating the positive and resisting your inner-outraged child.

Cold consideration–the best way to build your brand and reputation.

How do all those folks you follow earn that follow? I'm not talking about the clients and competitors you follow to stay up to date, but the ones you've never met, who are completely outside your geographic footprint, and who you will never sell yourself or a product to. Why follow someone like that?

Because they are sharing something you value, and on a regular basis. They are saying something that resonates with you, and you honor them with your attention. Why can't you do the same? You can, and since you're reading this book, you clearly want to—so why don't you?

If you've been in any sector of business for any period of time, you've undoubtedly developed a set of personal 'rules of thumb,' best practical practices, and 'I'll never do that agains.' So why don't you think a little bit deeper about why and how you created them, write them up blog-style, then post them to your blog, and promote them via your other feeds?

Just doing that, especially on LinkedIn, means you've made a conscious decision to join the Online Elite, the 1% of users who actually add to the value of social media. Do that regularly, and your ROTOMA can't help but build as more and more people recognize your expertise, and your name.

Say one 'smart' thing, and you are worth listening to. Say such things over and over again, adding *original* thinking to such incredibly regurgative media environment, and you're a capital 'E' Expert.

You know who gets paid more, asked to speak at industry gatherings, and is head and shoulders above the general population of folks who do what you do? Experts. How can you become one? One word (say it with me): ROTOMA.

The secret to great customer reviews.

Is there a secret to great customer reviews? Yes, and it's much easier to implement than you might expect. Question: When is your customer's enthusiasm the highest? After a great experience, right?

After you've done something awesome, your customer WANTS to support you and tell other people. This same method applies to those of us who want great recommendation and referral letters too. My rock band taught me this lesson many years ago, but this killer idea applies to every industry.

The rock band merchandise table— the ultimate voting booth.

Think of the last time you went to a concert. On the way out the door, after you experienced a (hopefully) great performance, you walked by the merchandise table (commonly known as a merch booth).

That's the place where the performers will sell CDs, clothing, posters, and the like. Many times, they'll be there to autograph the merchandise and chitchat with fans too. At this point, fans will "vote" on how they feel about the band's performance through spending money on merch.

Why do the performers go to the merchandise table immediately after the show? That's when the fans are still experiencing the afterglow of the concert. This is the absolute best time for someone to purchase something from you, and it will generally be the highest price you can charge for your merchandise too. The 'half-life' of this enthusiasm is extremely short and is almost non-existent after a week or so.

The next time you're at a concert, keep an eye out for this one very savvy marketing move: the location of the band's merch table. It's not off to the side, or some place where there's room for a crowd. Most times, it's right in the middle of the lobby or the exit aisles leading out of the venue. The merch table often creates a bottleneck, slowing the crowd down as they are on their way out. And it's supposed to.

Such exit bottlenecks are exactly where where bands and venues *want* the merchandise table to be set up. Why? Venues always want to attract great bands to play at their location, and if the band sells a lot of merchandise, everyone is happy. This setup is no accident—it's a band and festival satisfaction strategy from the get go.

How to get great reviews for your business by asking immediately.

"Ok," you might be thinking. "I'm not in a business where a performance can sell something for me." You're wrong. In your business, you're 'performing' constantly. Any time you're in the presence of your customers, your interactions with them are being judged, and their impression will influence others.

These performances, then, can help you ensure future revenue by letting the world know your customers are happy. After that interaction concludes, ask immediately for feedback, and if it's positive, request a great review from that customer. What's the key here, though? You need to ask immediately.

When your customers have a great experience, ask them right away to complete the review on the phone they're carrying with them, and request they use whatever ratings site you feel is most pertinent to your customers. We all need to use technology to our advantage in this respect.

Since everyone is connected to the Web constantly, how much time will it take your customer to do the review? 60-90 seconds, maybe? The secret to a great customer review in this case: being top of mind. Once he or she gets home—or even back into their car—the likelihood of a review dwindles substantially.

If you're running a retail establishment or restaurant, you need more than the obligatory "Review Us on Yelp," sticker. Have your server or staff person give your guests a gift certificate for themselves and a friend after the customers complete a review on their phones.

Your great reviews will skyrocket past your competitors. As long as they're at it, encourage the customers to talk about their great experience on Twitter, Facebook, or other social network of choice too. Consider providing another reward for this as well.

Reviews, referrals and recommendations are the life blood of ROTOMA.

If you're in the kind of business where public reviews are uncommon, but letters of recommendation or referrals are, this secret to great customer reviews is every bit as applicable.

After hearing great feedback from your customers, you should ask right away for a recommendation, referral letters, LinkedIn endorsements and connection, Facebook page 'likes'—literally anything you feel is appropriate and optimized for your ROTOMA strategy.

Looking back to my band days, oh how we would have killed for fan-generated Facebook Live videos, Instagram Stories, and tweets before, during and after our concerts. These exciting and incredibly popular services give us something we could never have had back in the day: a completely user-generated, uber enthusiastic marketing team that we didn't have to recruit, direct, or most importantly, pay.

Another major benefit to this approach is that as customers write recommendation or referral letters for you it forces them to crystallize their thoughts about your 'performance.'

In many ways, these customers will be writing a near perfect, user-oriented script they can then use to recommend you to others. The next time an acquaintance of theirs asks about you, they can cite the letter or even give it directly to someone on your behalf.

By asking for a review, reference, or referral, you've armed your best sales force (current customers) with everything they need to sell your services, and you don't even have to pay them a cent for doing so. A once-silent customer turned enthusiastic sales evangelist? That's another real-world example of ROTOMA in action.

Back catalog to the Future.

There's something the late, great Michael Jackson knew better than just about anyone: the value of an extensive back catalog.

The story I heard was that while on the set for the music video *Say Say Say*, a duet he sang in with Paul McCartney, during a conversation about the music business, Jackson turned to the ex-Beatle and calmly said, "I'm going to buy your songs." And he did, outbidding Paul McCartney himself, for a paltry $47MM in 1985. The value of that 'back catalog' publishing now? Searching online, I've found estimates of as high $1 Billion US.

What's your social media back catalog?

Are you viewing everything you post as valuable? You should be. Every photo, tweet, and especially blog post has a little bit of social media mojo associated with it. Over time, and when carefully cultivated, updated, and periodically re-posted, the mojo builds and builds, until it's truly monstrous—in a good way.

It's become a bit of a social media cliché: a stay-at-home mom, bored out of her mind, starts a blog about her personal passion. That blog finds an audience. Her posts add up, creating perennial interest and incrementally adding to her network of fans, until what was a passion project turns into a viable income. She then becomes the family's primary breadwinner, with her husband retiring early to become Mr. Mom and a key support as the Chairman of the BOD for her burgeoning online empire.

Yeah, it's a cliché. And her name is Ruth Soukup of livingwellspendingless.com.

Ruth's back catalog of social media content, stretching all the way to 2010, is filled with valuable of tips on balancing life and budget while creating a home filled with personal faith and family is worth a lot. So much so that my team chose to partner with her on a couple of 'strictly social' marketing initiatives.

Why? Because the value of her brand was burnished by her vast back catalog of social media activity. Her value to the agency and sponsoring brand was incredible because it was 100% REAL, 100% Ruth, and 100% sharable socially.

Soon, your back catalog will become your front man.

Every time you write, post, tweet, or like/comment/subscribe, you amplify your voice. Over time that voice accrues value. You may never want a national public profile, but how about one in your professional or personal niche?

What if, at the next conference or event you attend, people made the effort to cross the room specifically to meet you? Or what if you were asked to speak at that conference because your reputation proceeded you in conversations within your 'small world' professional niche?

Building your social media mojo can make such things happen—unless you're not doing anything to generate that mojo in the first place. Need an idea where to start? Check out *Unselfish Selfies* on page 189.

A simple pic, a comment with a few shoutouts, in 10 minutes your done—and just deposited a little bit of mojo in your social media/back catalog savings account—an account that accrues interest over time without you doing anything more than you've already done.

Wisdom in bulk:
3 valuable lessons from Costco.

In 2016, Costco rose yet again on the Fortune 500 list to number 15; a steady increase over the years. What can you learn from one of the world's largest companies that continues to get larger and larger? Here are three best practices you can start implementing today.

Lesson #1. Collect data.

Whenever you check out at Costco, you scan your membership card. Why does Costco do that? They build a database on you. They study what it is that you buy and when you buy it.

As a result, they're able to offer you— and people just like you— better products and services. Without having to ask you, they simply look at your behavior and they're able to offer you more of what you want, and stock fewer of the things that you don't.

What if you don't have a membership program, though? Ask. Ask again. And listen.

1. Ask your customers why they chose you. The best time to do this is when your customers are actually buying something from you, whether it's in person or online.

2. Another avenue is through surveys via mail, or email, or social media. Ask your customers why they chose you and ask your customers what they want from you in the future.

3. A critical way is by simply listening to your customers on social media. It's a really great way to keep your fingers on the pulse of your customers and key to retaining their business. Go a step further and listen to what it is that they're sharing, and make your decisions based on those things.

Lesson #2.
Offer FEWER / BETTER choices.

"Spencer, have you been in a Costco before? You're telling me that my business should offer FEWER choices? Look at this place!" Hold on a second, though. Let's zoom in:

Picture the toothpaste selection at Costco. You notice, that out of all the top brands out there, that only a few make the Costco cut. There's Crest, their Kirkland brand that they created themselves, and maybe a couple of specialty types. Why would they do this?

Costco knows their customers. Costco knows that their affluent customers have more money than they do time, so their customers don't want to make decisions. But they insist on quality. The implication of this is that by only offering you a couple of top-quality choices, Costco has already done all of the hard work. They say, "Look, regardless of what it is that you choose, you'll be making a great decision."

Lesson #3.
Guarantees that actually mean something.

Let's take a look at Costco's outstanding return policy:

On Membership

They'll refund your membership fee in full at any time if you're dissatisfied.

On Merchandise

They guarantee your satisfaction on every product they sell and will refund your purchase price with the following exceptions... (which include electronics, diamonds, alcohol, that kind of stuff). It doesn't get more clear, concise—or consumer satisfying—than that.

Can something as basic as a guarantee affect your ROTOMA? Ask Jlyne.

This is ROTOMA you can take to the bank.

MarketWatch, the respected national media outlet for all things business, takes a page from the ROTOMA playbook (see *Ask simple questions. Share smart answers.* page 119), lofts a slow pitch over the plate on Twitter, and Ms. Hanbeck swats it out of the park—for Costco. And what social media activity did Costco have to do to garner this 100% real, 100% sincere endorsement? NOTHING—except have a guarantee worth tweeting about.

So in this simple Twitter event we've got:

A. *MarketWatch* 'ROTOMA-ing' their social presence (actively)

B. Jlyne 'ROTOMA-ing' her social presence (actively)

C. Costco 'ROTOMA-ing' their social presence
(passively, but in the best way possible, via user-generated applause)

That's an amazing amount of ROTOMA, and it all came about because of a remarkable guarantee policy (that is literally worth remarking about).

So consider the ROTOMA-boosting potential that's folded into the ordinary 'cost of doing business' guarantees and warranties.

There are actually two distinct kinds:

1. The guarantee that everybody has.

2. The guarantee customers actually believe (and that customers are willing to put their personal names on the social media line to tout to their network of followers, family, and friends).

Such 'no questions asked' policies create a bonanza of social media goodwill. When you offer guarantees or assurances, make sure that you honor and immediately follow up on them.

Satisfied customers, given that kind of delightful post-purchase service are the best social media evangelists you can ask for. They offer the very best possible kind of ROTOMA: personal endorsement. And they keep you 'top of mind'—*but all you had to do was keep the promise you already made.*

Ask simple questions.
Share smart answers.

"I just don't have that much to say." That's a sentence that's been said by countless people who *know* they should actively participate on social media but *don't*.

For every blogger or tastemaker who loves opining at the drop of a tweet, there's a vast majority of lurkers who can't be bothered—or more likely, suffer from "I'm no expert" syndrome (a topic addressed throughout this book).

The fact is, you need to get over it. If you want to ever achieve your best possible online presence and get the all the profile- and career-enhancing benefits it has to offer, you have to add to the conversation in a meaningful way.

But just like any casual gathering, it's not necessary to have a fully baked, world-shaking, original idea to share. In fact, the best conversations often start very simply, with a really good question.

I met my friend Diana Pastrana at a recent 1 Million Cups meeting in Madison, and she shared her absolute joy about an encounter at a coffee shop just minutes before.

Seems she was stood up for a coffee date but stayed around because she couldn't help eavesdropping in on a fascinating conversation going on between a number of older (possibly retired) gentlemen.

It all started with a simple, really great question:

Who is your favorite romantic male character in literature?

Evidently that got everyone talking and provided Diana with a truly delightful morning coffee experience. BTW: for the record, the consensus appeared to be coalescing around Pride & Prejudice's Fitzwilliam Darcy. Good choice, IMO.

You don't have to have the answer.
Your network will—but you get the credit.

As mentioned elsewhere, the magazine *Premier Guitar* really has its act together on social. The following example of a Facebook BYO party is proof of what this concept is all about.

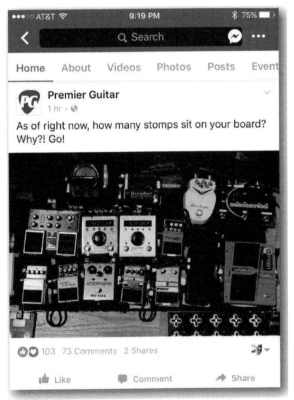

Asking electric players about their pedal boards is like asking grandparents about their grandkids.

The cool thing is not the question, but the comments: 73 and climbing. That's 73 fans telling *PG* they are truly top of mind. Add to that the Likes and all the non-responding lurkers (like me), and you've got some serious ROTOMA building—and all for a simple, but 100% audience-relevant question, and the user-generated answers that it provoked.

Did you know LinkedIn is one of social's most happening party spots?

It is. Just go to any LinkedIn group, and you'll see such lively discussions happening many times every day. A recent query in the Social Media Marketing group "What is your favorite social media scheduling/management tool?" was simple, relevant to the group, and also a little bit of personal promotion for the asker, Hilary Meyerson of Little Candle Media.

This simple, sincere question yielded 867 posted answers and 471 likes (at time of writing). All for a 'what do you guys think?' question. And get this, even though it was posted for two months ago (as of this writing), it was still generating answers from members of the group. Evidently, that's a question that's continues to drive conversation. Good job, Hilary!

Now imagine someone collated and analyzed the answers, and provided that intel as part of their personal feeds. That's valuable information, worth sharing, AGAIN.

One question.
Four significant posting opportunities.

Post #1: Ask the question.

"What is your favorite social media scheduling/management tool?"

Post #2: Report Interim Findings / Re-ask the question.

"Wow, right now <SOLUTION A> is leading the pack, with 30% of you pointing to it as your favorite. <SOLUTION B> isn't very far behind, though. Are there any other tools that we should be considering?"

Post #3: Report Final Findings.

"This has been so great—input from over <XXX> people from <XX countries>! The final tally as of today is 37% recommend <SOLUTION A>, 26% <SOLUTION B>, and a new tool called <SOLUTION C> appears to be a strong contender with a solid 14% even though they only just launched in January."

"The rest of the responses mentioned <SOLUTION D>, <SOLUTION E>, <SOLUTION F>, and<SOLUTION G> to account for the full 100%. Looks like these are the tools everyone should be considering. Thanks for the help!"

Pro-Post #4: Blog the results.

Now you have something really worth sharing: actual numbers and expert recommendations, plus first-name access to experts that can add richness to your findings. Taking these and turning them into a cross-postable blog post paints you as a go-to expert in this area. **All because of one simple question.**

Using social media to make your clients look GREAT.

Quick question for you—what's easier—getting new clients or taking care of your existing ones? Of course the answer is the latter. It's always easier to retain existing business because they already know and trust you. So, how are you showing your existing clients that you care about them?

What if there's a way that you could do this for free, so you can be sure that they know that you really care, and that they can actually see that you're doing this in public? Let's pretend social media didn't exist at all. How would you normally do this? **How would you normally brag about your clients in public?**

Pick up any edition of a major newspaper like the *Wall Street Journal* and you'll find them. Full page, full color ads paid for by one company, but touting the success of another. Ever stop to think how much an ad like this costs? Well, I asked, and was amazed at the answer.

To run a single page / full color ad just once costs $192,921. That's right, almost $200,000 for a 'feel good' ad featuring an important client, but without an offer, discount, or even a basic call to action driving to a website or anything else. There's got to be a better, more affordable way to do this. And with social media, there is.

What if you don't have a $192+K for a full-color Wall Street Journal ad?

Use your existing—and free—social media channels to highlight your clients. Look for good news that's out there right now that you can highlight. ASK your clients next time you're talking to them, "Hey what awards have you won recently? What can I help you amplify? Are you particularly excited about any recent achievements?"

Use the existing thing that you own to tell your audience about how proud you are of a client that you have. When you do this post, be sure that you tag your client so they can see it, and they can tell you how much they appreciate that you've done that.

Shine the spotlight via social media— on them, not you.

Every trade show, ground breaking, grand opening, significant hire, new biz win, and major milestone is an opportunity to spotlight your clientele. And don't be afraid to get personal.

Let's consider a tough sales business: car insurance. It's a cutthroat business with everyone promising lower rates and 'untouched by human hands' service you can access online, any time. What's an old-school insurance agent supposed to do to counteract the TV commercial budget Flo is prepared to blow? Get personal.

Here's just one idea for any agent who's paper still lists the names of students who make the high school honor roll: pay special attention to the freshman and sophomore class recipients, then tweet / Insta / Facebook out a photo of the listings in the paper with the the kids' names highlighted.

Got some spare time? Do the research and customize each photo with a single student's @ handle. Why? Mom and Dad, who love to see their stellar student recognized (and follow their kid's social feeds), are likely to appreciate your amplification of their child's accomplishment. And they are the ones buying insurance coverage—for their soon to be driving Freshman or Sophomore.

Labor intensive? Sure. But if you don't have it in your budget, you better take it out of time. And for heaven's sake, make sure it's personal, and from you yourself. That robo-mailed crap you send me is worse than worthless. All it is for me and many, is expensive recycling fodder. But an image you've spent time on touting my kid? That's ROTOMA.

Ephemeral vs. Evergreen.

With Snapchat and other applications and websites leading the charge of Ephemeral marketing, it's a good time to step back, breathe deep, and ask one very important question for your brand or business:

What's more important: Ephemeral or Evergreen?

The Three B's—**Budget**, **Bandwidth**, and **Brand Relevance**—have long been the primary limiting parameters for any marketing campaign. The challenge has always been to balance all three to achieve the biggest brand bang for the buck.

Enter the rise of ephemeral marketing (EpM).

Designed to be millennial sexy and take advantage of the currently hottest social media channels, ephemeral marketing is literally here today and gone tomorrow. Think Snapchat. That undeniably popular app enables the creation of an incredibly interesting video *which then disappears within hours*. That powerful—yet ephemeral—concept takes FOMO (Fear of Missing Out) and turns it up to 11. That is the strength of EpM, and its undeniable weakness.

• Snapchat et al are the perfect channels for ephemeral products and their equally fickle audiences.

• Fast food, fads, or fashion? Perfect.

• Huge millennial audience? Worth thinking about as a part of your marketing mix.

• Armed with a fat budget administered by a fast-fingered digital team that is built to run at the speed of NOW! EpM might be good idea.

**But what about the 90+ percent of businesses and brands
that aren't any of the above?
That's a rhetorical question you can answer yourself.**

Some brands are pioneering the EpM space.
But should yours?

I'd rather have you focus on an 'Evergreen' marketing philosophy that embraces a tight brand discipline which prizes a consistent message consistently delivered over whatever ephemeral shiny object is the 'It' app of today. After all it wasn't so long ago that we were all supposed to be 'kicking butt on Vine.' Then Twitter bought Vine, then pulled 'em out by the roots. Ouch.

**What's Evergreen?
Whatever marketing devices are
always relevant to your brand,
and consistently available to your customer.**

An example of Evergreen marketing:
Online video.

Online video is the gift that keeps on giving. And the best part: it provides you with visual and messaging elements that can be cut and re-cut into whatever length and style you need. A 60-second Instagram version? No problem. You have the elements, now just adjust the conceptual style to meet the platform, re-edit, and you're good to go.

There's one word that content marketers love: library. A library of ownership-clear motion / still photography and graphic elements that are one resize away from posted is pure gold for content marketers who are continually asked to do more, faster, and with less.

If there's a long-term future for Ephemeral marketing, prove it.

"If all your friends jumped of a cliff, would you?" I used to hear that every time I did something ill-considered or darn near life threatening. It's an incredibly apt question to ask re: EpM too.

I'm not saying not to do it. But just like a 40+ year-old Dad wearing skinny jeans, maybe it's not the best fit for you, your brand, and especially, your marketing budget. Just because your brand doesn't do it today doesn't mean you can't in the future once this nascent field has proven itself a little more—and in the only way that really matters: @ the cash register.

While EpM may be fantastic in terms of ROTOMA, it's essential to at least question the return on investment on content that mimics the lifetime of a fruit fly.

Here today and gone tomorrow? Is that a long-term strategy you or your company can embrace? A comprehensive ROTOMA strategy demands you, at the very least, ask the question.

Serve sushi, not Clickbait.

In the world of social media, the term 'clickbait' has become a go-to descriptor for that which is designed to grab your eye, garner your click, and deliver you elsewhere. It's also got a bit of an aroma associated with it related to its propensity to over-promise and under-deliver.

Clickbait can be a headline:

Amazing but true!
Supermodel uses all-butter diet to melt weight away!

A listicle:

What happened to the Hotty?
15 gorgeous stars who look terrible now!

Or a bait and switch come on:

I made six million with just one blog post!
Find out how NOW!

Want a nearly infallible way to identify clickbait?
Just count the exclamation points!!!!!!!

Working in marketing and advertising, my professional Twitter feed is filled with clickbait. Every once and a while I go on a tear and un-follow the most egregious abusers (yeah, that's why I un-followed you), but they still find a way back in. But this is not about them. It's about Scott Galloway, one of the very best sushi-masters in the marketing industry.

The Professor doesn't make sushi.
But he tweets it.

If you don't know Scott Galloway, founder of digital intel group L2 and Clinical Professor of Marketing at NYU's Stern School of Business, go to YouTube right now and search 'scott galloway winners and losers' and watch any of the videos there. The dude is a riot of information and deeply considered opinion, and IMHO, his 'Winners & Losers' video series is must-see social media marketing TV.

This guy call you a 'loser?' You've arrived!

But it's his Twitter feed I want to focus on. When I call Professor Galloway a sushi-master what I mean is that his 140-character tweets, which often link directly to his content elsewhere, are like bite-sized pieces of magnificently curated fish flesh. And if you're like me, you can't eat just one, and you're in for the full meal.

Take a look at this tweet series
re: the 2017 Cannes Lion Festival–

Clickbait?
Not when you're hungry for what's being served.

I'm not saying you're going to bite on any of the above—but I certainly did. Why? Because the topic, the tone, and even the tiny bit of substance offered is perfectly tuned to my taste. And the fact that I'm squarely in his target of marketing pros, let's just say he knows his audience.

After years of watching, listening, and learning from Professor Galloway's work online, I know his personality and perspicuity. He's got data I find enlightening, and an attitude I find entertaining. He serves me the sushi I love, so every time one of his creations shows up in feed, I bite.

Clickbait = sizzle - steak.
Sushi = sizzle + steak...err...spicy tuna.

One man's clickbait may be another man's dinner, but my larger point is about the person in the kitchen. While I'm sure, based on volume produced alone, the Professor has some T.A.s working under his direction, the quality of the content and its tone and voice is clearly his. Watch just two 'Winners & Losers' videos and you'll see, hear, and completely understand what I mean.

Sushi packs high quality content, curation, talent, and expertise into a bite-sized delight. Clickbait is like cotton candy, more fluff and flash than food. The #1 way to keeping feeding your followers' feeds? Serve 'em sushi.

FAQ You.

The simple FAQ, Frequently Asked Questions, is one of the greatest written tools ever invented by humankind. I'm not kidding. Introduced in the early years of text-only websites, the FAQ was an easy-to-find, easy-to-write piece of content that did one thing perfectly: answer users' first, basic, yet incredibly salient questions.

If you actively think about any sales meeting or networking event you've been involved with, they are very likely to start out with these mandatories (or some variation thereof):

What's your name? What shall I call you?

What do you do (implied: "Please explain it in a way I can easily understand)?

How can you help me?

How are you different than others that I perceive to be just like you?

How much does it (your product) / your services cost?

People ask such basic question because they legitimately want to know the answers. They are 'pulling' the answers out of you, to get the information they want without any kind of sales varnish. In doing so, your social media audience is pointing you to vein full of rich posting opportunities—but are you mining it as a part of your ROTOMA strategy?

If it's frequently asked,
It's frequently postable.

There's what you want to say. And what they (your audience) wants to know. My money is on the latter. By answering those FAQ questions in a variety of creative ways and via non-standard social media channels, you can fill your feed with content that you *know* there's an audience for *because they keep asking you for it.*

A brand like ClosetMaid, the manufacturer of home organization products and systems, is faced with these kinds of challenges on a daily basis, and around the clock. No matter how good their enclosed assembly instructions may be (and they are quite good), more and more people are turning to YouTube as the very first stop in their quest for installation information.

Don't treat YouTube like a channel.
It's your 24/7/365 TV network.

The solution? A YouTube-based (and cross-posted from the ClosetMaid website) webseries called *QuickTips*. The series turns what was a written FAQ page into a menu of quick bite videos that are perfect for the weekend handy-man or -woman.

Crafted to be as slim as possible, yet still containing all the information needed to answer the question, most *QuickTips* are well under the 'I'm getting bored' 3-minute barrier. And since smart phones are becoming the de facto onsite resource for the active installer, they are also optimized for mobile devices, with easy-to-read-even-without-glasses graphics and information.

Here's just one example that my team and I created that answers the eternal question of 'What's the right hardware for my type of wall.' It's a critical question to ask *before* starting the installation as anyone who has watched a carefully installed closet system pull straight out of the wall can attest, so we created a user-friendly video answer for use on ClosetMaid's *QuickTips* YouTube channel, their website, PowerPoint sales presentations, and just about anywhere online capable of serving up video.

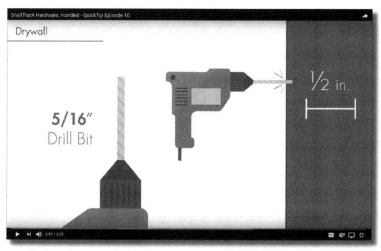

It doesn't get much simpler, or more user valuable, than this.

The entire series covers ClosetMaid's FAQs one at a time, and maintains it's user relevance by never veering into any kind of sales pitch. It's a pure goodwill-generating give that helps differentiate ClosetMaid from their competitors, and add value to every product in their inventory. And the fact that one of them, *How to Design a Closet* has racked up an impressive 52,399 views (at the time of writing) and growing shows that yes, it is a frequently asked question worth answering.

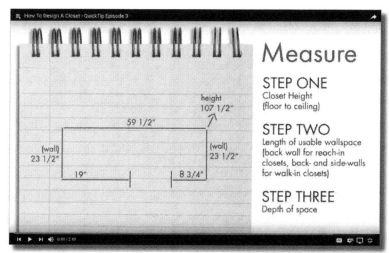

Best way to plant the seed for your brand at the point-of-purchase?
Answer the questions they have BEFORE that purchase.

The *QuickTips* webseries is just one of the 'shows' playing all day, every day on ClosetMaid's YouTube TV station. The audience is there, racking up views (and valuable brand engagements) whenever they want or need it. ClosetMaid created the videos just once—but benefits every time anyone presses play.

Once you have the video— edit for everywhere.

I am a big believer in the idea that 'Video is the King of Content,' but for different reasons than most adherents to this particular faith. Yes, it catches eyeballs (and I love it for that), but as a Content Strategist, I *really* love it for its incredible flexibility.

A finished longform video (say, over 2 minutes) is like a side of beef. It can be cut and re-cut to serve up just about any video dish you can think of.

Need a shortform video for any number of the social channels out there that require it? If you have the longform, get editing. Once the footage is in-library, it's off to the races. Never, ever go cheap on shooting footage. As long as you steer clear of too-trendy fashions, color palettes and hairstyles, high-quality digital video has a shelf life of…. **forever**.

ROTOMA / HOW

Now that you know you should be social and what to be social about, it's time to take a look at how you can ROTOMA while maintaining a full time job and a balanced personal life.

This section takes a look at some completely doable techniques and posting styles that can help max out your ROTOMA efforts without stressing you out.

Step #1: One step.

Start with the basics.

For the sake of this discussion, let's assume you have the bare minimum for any ROTOMA strategy: pages on LinkedIn and Facebook. Experts battle it out daily on which is more important, but the fact is, both are equally critical keystones to have it place before starting anything else. Why? Because one, the other, or both are the 'where' to which your ROTOMA strategy will be directing any generated interest (assuming you don't also have a website or blog).

For many people, these two sites are the first search stop before any engagement, and if you're not there, you're missing a great opportunity to make a first impression.

Seriously. If only all All-Star awards were this easy.

Do you have a LinkedIn All-Star Profile? Why not?

One of nefarious techniques LinkedIn uses to get users to completely fill out their profiles is to award 'soft' achievements for section completion. It's a gamification technique—that works. That illusive 'All-Star Profile' rating is worth achieving too. Why? LinkedIn, like it or not, has become a daily intel resource for just about everybody in business.

It's more than a résumé because it can be a venue for you to demonstrate your expertise. It's a minimally invasive matchmaker, too, as it's always suggesting others you might be interested in 'Linking' to. And it's, without a doubt, an incredible tool for sales prospecting, job hunting, 'just checking them out before we meet' 411 and more. No wonder Spencer predicts that it will become "the #1 source for business intelligence" in the future. From my point-of-view, that future is NOW.

So if LinkedIn is such a powerful tool for business, is there any reason you shouldn't have an 'All-Star' profile. Well, Federal Witness Protection program participants probably shouldn't. But for everybody else, it's a no-brainer, and an easy, yet critical first step in any ROTOMA strategy.

Pick a channel—and master it.

Some recommend blogging first. But me, I recommend dessert first. If blogging is fun and you love writing deep, meaningful takes on the things that interest you about your industry sector, by all means, start a blog. But if you hate writing an email, I'd start some place more amenable, like a social media channel that aligns with your interests. Here are some examples:

Love photography? **Instagram**.

Opinionated, but hate writing? **Twitter**.

Deep thinker / Thought Leader? **Start a blog**.

By aligning your social media activity with an interest you enjoy, you're far more likely to keep doing it. This persistence is absolutely fundamental to keeping your face, ideas, and brand (personal or otherwise) on top of your audiences' minds. This primary channel becomes your de facto Flagship (see *What's your Flagship?*, page 77), serving as the strategic hub for everything else you do in social media

One of the primary rules of ROTOMA: quantity is quality. Just be sure it quality, relevant content. Just remember: spammy, overtly salesy or poorly considered content is rarely appreciated, and can negatively affect your image online and in real life.

Cross-post where possible.

There was a time when cross-posting was frowned upon. Some still claim it's a version of spam, redundantly polluting the web with identical content. To that, I ask "Why are there so many libraries." They all have the same books. Why isn't there just one?

Ridiculous, right?

Rather than create content that accrues value only to the semi- or completely walled gardens of LinkedIn, Facebook, Medium, et al, ROTOMA rightly demands that you seek to create content that accrues value to you. I can't assume that a post to my blog will be seen by site-centric audiences. Therefore, I post them, sometimes in minimally modified versions, to all the above, and from within the LinkedIn / Facebook / Medium site itself (to ensure maximum exposure). Why? Because I can't possibly be 'top of mind' unless I am. A blog snippet, with image, goes to Instagram, Twitter, and other short form channels. But full versions of the post that originated at my blog are also posted wherever I can amplify the message.

There may be legitimate SEO reasons for not cross-posting if you're an institution like *The New York Times*, but if you're working to maximize your ROTOMA, there's no reason not to cross-post like crazy.

Wouldn't you like your book to be in every library there is? Well, the internet is not, despite the wishes of many, a single library that everyone can access anytime, anywhere. You need to be where your audience is—and your audience is everywhere. Facebook-oriented people may spend the vast majority of their social activity within Facebook. Same with LinkedIn-oriented folks. If you spent as much time as you should to create that ROTOMA-enhancing blog post, shouldn't it be conveniently accessible to those site-centric folks? Yes, it should.

You can't optimize what you don't have.

Too many people worry about the wrong things. Example: giving one iota of attention to something like search engine optimization before you have even one post to optimize. Yes, there are best practices (and a metric shite ton of optimizers out there). But you have to crawl before you walk before you run before you strive for a slot at the Olympics.

Yes, you have to 'see it to be it.' But if you're like me and most others, you also have to 'fake it to make it.' What's the best time to post your first meaningful 'thought leadership' to LinkedIn to ensure maximum engagement? Right now. You've got to get in the pool before you start refining your stroke. The more you do, the stronger you'll get, and the faster you'll swim. **But it all starts by getting in the pool.**

Free Like–the incredible power of a simple 'thumbs-up.'

Now that it's possible to buy 'likes' by investing in paid reach on social media, some brands have almost completely abandoned their organic social media efforts. They're focusing on optimizing their ads and targeting the right demographics, and they're obsessed with the ROI of each like they receive.

Anyone who has just run a major Facebook advertising campaign can probably spit out the average cost of each like gained throughout the campaign. Sure, that's the cost of buying a like. But what's the cost of giving a like?

Social media is still, at its core, a community. No matter which platform you're on, it's a way to use technology to have one-on-one conversations at scale. And conversations require two-way communication.

Think about the best conversationalist you know: Is she a great talker, or is she actually a great listener who makes you feel valued when you speak with her?

> *"One of the most sincere forms of respect is actually listening to what another has to say."* -Bryant H. McGill

The best social media strategy puts more emphasis on listening and engaging with others' content than it does on promoting its own.

The policies of Reddit, the social network focused on sharing, rating, and discussing news and other website content, illustrate the crucial role listening plays in social media.

It's almost impossible to spam a forum on Reddit because you have to earn your way into the community by liking, commenting, and appreciating others' content before you can start sharing your own. If you haven't proved your commitment to the community and to supporting others with upvotes and comments, most of your own posts will never get approval.

What Reddit understands is there's a huge value in protecting the entire ecosystem it has created. People use Reddit because they trust the conversations that are going on there. You cannot succeed on Reddit unless you are a true Reddit native.

And even though other platforms aren't nearly as quick to ban you from their community as Reddit if you blatantly try to use the platform for your own gain, the principles are the same. You can't truly succeed on any social media platform unless you bring real value to the community. Think about it from a psychological perspective.

People often fear putting themselves out there. So when they finally put in the effort to share a piece of their own original work, but no one reacts to it, it's almost worse than if someone said something mean.

"The deepest principle in human nature is the craving to be appreciated."
- Harvard psychologist William James

Social media offers you a platform to satisfy the deepest principle in human nature. And the best part of it? It doesn't cost a thing.

You can't underestimate the value of expressing your honest appreciation for the content that people in your network are producing.

I've noticed that many people who are wonderful listeners in person haven't connected the dots to realize that social media is all about listening as well. The number of people who view a post compared to the number who like it is drastically different.

I'll see people at networking events who will say, "I saw that thing you put out on LinkedIn the other day." I'll say, "Oh you did? I didn't see you like it or comment on it." They'll respond, "Oh I don't really 'like' things on social media. I don't do that."

Part of me wants to shake them. Many people have this hesitation to signal that they like something or support it on social media. They prefer to just observe. Sometimes, they're too busy putting out their own content to spend any time interacting with others.

This is a huge opportunity.

If you're the one organization that's actively engaging in and liking other people's stuff and letting them know that you value it, you will become valuable to them.

My own experience with Instagram proves the value of building your social strategy around giving likes first. My personal account has grown to about 4,000 followers after 400+ posts. The posts reflect both my personal interests and some insights on social media marketing, and I've never followed a specific strategy to gain more followers.

Another account I own, Law Marketing, has many of the same posts as my personal account. But on Law Marketing, I hit 3,000+ followers with only 50 posts. Since the content is similar, I attribute that difference to my activity on each page.

On my personal page, I've focused more on putting out my own content and waiting for friends to react. On Law Marketing, I made a concerted effort to find other accounts producing content that I valued and to show them my appreciation. I would set a timer on my phone for five minutes, and then I would search law-related hashtags and spend that five minutes liking other people's posts.

My strategy worked because of a basic fact of human nature. When we receive a compliment, we usually view the giver of the compliment in a positive light.

The world is full of people who
are great at receiving compliments.
What the world needs is more people
who give great compliments.

It used to be a lot harder to publicly show your support and appreciation for your clients or partners in business. Before social media existed, taking out an ad in a magazine, newspaper, or TV network was the only way to brag about your clients or partners publicly, and it was prohibitively expensive. As I talked about in *Using social media to make your clients look GREAT (*page 123), a half page full-color ad in the Wall Street Journal costs $192,921 for one day. Who's got budget for that these days?

With social media, we can help other people feel good by publicly acknowledging their good work. And we can do that for free. It's the modern-day equivalent of showing up to an open house to fill the room and show your support. By listening to the voices in your network, showing your support, and helping to amplify their voice, you will earn their loyalty, respect, and engagement, and it won't cost you a thing.

The cost of giving a like is nothing,
but the value of a like is priceless.

Killer Cereal.

The when, why, and how of social is everywhere. Hundreds of Top 5/10/50 lists of 'Must dos' to build your social presence. Millions of words (and pictures) telling when to post, where to post, and how to post. But there's surprisingly little about the most important content question out there: What to Post?

That is probably the #1 friction point for people wanting to become active on social media. "What should I actually be blogging/tweeting/podcasting/YouTubing about?" is the question that stops too many from actually getting out there by going social. And you know what? It's a really good question, and one the should be answered strategically before picking up a pencil or hitting the keyboard to craft your first piece of content.

Strategic is a word that delights people like me—but terrifies or mystifies others. I love it because it gives me, the content creator, parameters. **In the Creative world, if anything is possible, nothing is.** Too many options and possibilities can lead to analysis paralysis. But if Twitter only allows 140 characters, that's not so hard, right?

It's about the cereal, not the box.

The fact is, the vast majority of social media conversation is about 'the box.' What I'm talking about here is the cereal that goes in it: The actual content of your content marketing. Listicles are a form. Blog posts are a venue. Slideshows are a visual style.

Yes, each of these forms are legitimate, and should be optimized for SEO, friction-less clickthrough, and maximum reader engagement, but for crying out loud, don't live your Creative life like you're just waiting to be replaced by Artificial Intelligence (AI). I, for one, don't welcome our robot overlords.

As a writer, I hate the word 'content.' It's a word non-writers use as a catchall for 'stuff to fill the box' (and in many cases they really mean 'box,' as in text box, database fields, or wireframe copy blocks).

To call it 'content' diminishes the role stories play in transmitting information, attracting attention, and causing engagement strategies to actually engage readers/viewers, and further devalues the role of the writer in identifying, crafting, and optimizing the story to do all the above.

But it's also shorthand for all those things SEO-optimizers, clickthrough fetishists and customer-journey shamans can't do yet, but desperately need. The boxes they build need a constant supply of killer cereal.

So what's your cereal? Your true story.

What's your true story? That's a topic for another book, and the basis for my NonFiction Branding™ approach. It stipulates that your personal brand is inextricably based on your *true story*—and that the essence of that story should align perfectly with who you are, what you do, and the unique way you do it.

Think of a brand that you love. Any brand. Could be a product, service—or professional football team. Why do you love it? Not buy it, but love it. Answer that question about yourself/your company, and you've identified a story worth telling and showing via social media.

Social is about showing.

Every person, product, service, and company has a story to tell, and the very best marketers never, ever stop telling some version of it. That story: their own, distinct truth.

Carex Consulting is a career matchmaking firm that relies on a steady stream of top performing 'graduates' from a specific local company (Company X), then finds the right fit for not only those candidates, but also their corporate clients who want such battle-tested performers for their organizations.

In the old days of strictly traditional media, Carex may have placed a billboard in close proximity to that high-turnover company in order to get their message out to potential candidates.

But these are the brave new days of social. How could Carex work to become 'top of mind' for any soon-to-be or already ex-Company X employee? How could they possibly use social media to get their message out to potential candidates before, during, and after their transition out of said company? By taking a page out of @katiecosplays playbook:

44,000 followers and counting—
that's massive ROTOMA for herself—and Workfront.

This is how social media works. Katie gets a new job, and she's naturally excited about it, so she shares her joy with her friends and followers on Instagram. Yea, Katie! But also a big 'Yea' for Workfront.

Katie is already proving her value to her brand-new employer in a single photo. Count the number of references (direct and indirect) to Workfront.

1. Workfront logo on building
(Wow, they are established enough to own a building.)

2. Workfront logo on lanyard
(Casually embracing their newest employee.)

3. Katie tags @workfront in her post,
closely associated with an assortment of love-oriented emojis.

4. Katie raves about her excitement for Workfront

5. Note the comment from her follower 'eraru.'
He quietly endorses not only Katie's employment decision,
but Workfront's service platform.

And in terms of engagement? 601 Likes in just one day? Nice. Add in all the lurkers, and Workfront's got some really great ROTOMA for a single post that cost them absolutely nothing.

Buried lede: Katie's Instagram follower count (at time of writing): nearly of 44,000. Cosplaying as major ROTOMA technique? I guess so.

Wow. Workfront, Katie already deserves a raise.

As a company, what it you could multiply this ROTOMA-generating technique times the number of people you employ. Sure, some will do it better than others (and some should probably not be doing it at all), but just imagine the amount of authentic ROTOMA you'd build to your brand.

***I'll say it again: that's the way social works.
Is it working like that for you?***

This is Ninja level technique.

Back to Carex Consulting. They have an entire marketing plan filled with the regular blocking and tackling necessary to get their message to their audiences, but when it comes to infiltrating the vast community of ex-Company Xers, a technique like this is totally ninja.

Here's how I recommended it could work for them:

1. Place a candidate at a new job.

2. Ask them to grab a selfie in front of a distinct landmark associated with their new company (logoed building, exterior sign, conference room, etc.).

3. Ask that new employee to post the selfie to their feeds with the following hashtags: #1stDayNewGig #thxCarex.

And that's it. The post will instantly enter that person's social network, which undoubtedly includes many current or recent Company X employees. Now when such employees are ready to leave, or get churned out, guess what placement company is 'top of mind' with them? That's right, Carex Consulting. Get in, leave your calling card, and exit without leaving a trace. Brilliant social tactic? *Hai!*

Best way to begin? Start at the end.

What is it about your product, service, or self that you'd like your social audience to not only understand but believe? What's the takeaway you hoping to leave firmly entrenched in the mind of every reader/viewer? Here are a few for your consideration:

- That's a really smart/interesting/novel take.
- The creator of this post has great taste and a far-seeing radar.
- This person sorts through the crap and always delivers gold.
- What a great summary of a complicated topic.

"What do I want my audience to takeaway from this?" Answering that question before starting is a great way to focus the post while putting yourself into an audience-relevance mindset. What may have been an 'I' idea (as in "*I* want to say this") suddenly becomes a far more audience relevant 'You' takeaway (as in "Here's what *you* can do today").

If you've ever clicked on a link entitled something like "5 fast ways you can improve your site in 5 minutes," you have experienced this "Not I, You" orientation in action. It focuses the post on 'You' user benefit, all the while demonstrating 'I' expertise. You provide value. You demonstrate mastery of the post topic. You raise your profile, not by "look at me," but with "here's my gift to you."

Good things. Small packages. Big ROTOMA.

And the crazy thing is just how small that gift can be. Prime example: a simple Facebook Like. While Spencer goes deeper on this subject (see *Free Like*, page 145), my point is pretty simple: a nanosecond of activity on your part has the potential to generate an outsized response from its recipient. Ever get a Like on any social channel from a long, lost high school buddy, and then reconnect in some way? That's ROTOMA, baby.

Personal Branding Power Hour– a 60-minute strategy to social success.

As stated elsewhere *(Ed. Note:* and ad nauseum), I used to be a very, very minor rock star. Our band, Myopic Son, had the opportunity to play Summerfest, the Hard Rock Café, dozens of colleges, and hundreds of other gigs around the Midwest.

At almost every show we played, people would come up and say, "You guys are great. I listen to your album all the time." I'd reply, "Really? Until you just told me, I had no idea." Isn't that funny? Not until the right opportunity (being in the same room with us after a show where we performed) would people tell us how much they enjoyed what we did.

This same phenomenon happens today, too, and you don't need to be a proper rock star to experience it. Social media is the greatest mechanism ever invented for you to become known to your target market, and if you use social media the way I describe below, you'll be receiving accolades in real life from your fans, too.

Like anything else worth pursuing, this is going to take some work. If you invest one hour per business day (three 20-minute chunks each), following the formula I'm giving you here, your personal brand will start to explode on social media. Think of it as your Personal Branding Power Hour.

I personally do this first thing each morning and move through the three 20-minute sections consecutively. You may prefer to do them all at night or disperse the chunks throughout the day. Regardless, do what's best for you and start building momentum. You'll eventually form a habit and very quickly be off to the races.

Here's how the three sections break down:

- First 20 minutes—**Write**

- Second 20 minutes—**Get Social**

- Third 20 minutes—**Go to School**

Here are the steps in more detail. But before you start, a quick mechanical component:

Be very, very strict about the 20-minute limit on each activity. Set a timer, and when it goes off, you're done. Why is this important? The 20-minute increments (especially the second one) can easily expand to a half hour or more. We need you to associate, in your mind, this Personal Branding Power Hour as exactly that—an hour you invest in yourself. No more, no less.

If you're a big productivity dork like me, you get bonus points if you spend this hour on a treadmill desk or some equivalent form of exercise. Imagine, before breakfast each day—at a 3 mph pace on a walking treadmill—you'll already have walked 6,000 steps AND invested an hour in your personal brand. Remember, the asset that is your personal brand will only get more valuable over time.

1st 20 minutes–
Write.

At 5:15 a.m. each business day, I receive an email from Help A Reporter Out (HARO), a free service that matches a writer from a publication with a source. It's what I've used to earn features/quotes in Forbes, Entrepreneur, Inc., Money Magazine, Costco Connection, and dozens of others. I also credit it with giving me the necessary chops to earn a column with both *InBusiness* and *The Huffington Post*.

Aside from the obvious publicity/PR aspect, there's a tremendous advantage to the free service—a writer is sharing the news with you before it happens. Why is this important?

What's the hardest thing about writing? Staring at a blank screen thinking, "What should I write?"

With HARO, a writer is cueing you with a question you simply need to answer. After answering 240-plus queries, I've found it to be—by far—the best way to know what to write. Check out HARO for topic ideas, start writing for 20 minutes each business day, and you'll start your Personal Branding Power Hour with a bang.

2nd 20 minutes–
Get Social.

Grasping this concept alone will make the time you've invested reading this chapter worth it. How can YOU use social media effectively? Two keys:

1. Have a strategy
2. Have a list of priorities listed in descending order

Here's the strategy I use that you can consider using too: social media is the greatest means ever invented to have meaningful conversations at scale, and you should maximize the time you spend having meaningful conversations.

What does this mean?

It means that due to the asynchronous nature of social media you can batch your communications together when it's convenient for you. Also, because the vast majority of social media communications are in the public eye, those not directly involved in the conversation can observe what's happening.

Here's how that breaks down priorities-wise, then:

1. Acknowledge those that have mentioned you or shared something of yours.

2. Share the thing you've written in the first 20-minute Personal Branding Power Hour session.

3. Help other people look good using your social media channels.

Here are the individual priorities in more detail.

Priority 1– Acknowledge

Depending on how active you are on social media, this could be very quick or rather involved. If you've just started with the Personal Branding Power Hour, it's possible you have no mentions. Don't fret, though. As you step up priority Nos. 2 and 3, you'll have more and more people acknowledging you.

Why?

When people use their social media platforms to say something nice about you or share something of yours, it's really, really good etiquette to thank them.

The most popular post I've ever written on LinkedIn has been shared 116 times by people with whom I'm connected, and over 800 times by people I don't know. For those I know—and therefore could see the share—I individually thanked every single person. Why wouldn't I? They're helping tell their connections about something I created.

Priority 2– Share what you've created

In your first 20-minute session, you entered rarified air. You became part of the 1% of people online who actually create content. By becoming part of this 1%, you by default become a voice of your industry. Ever wonder, "What should I share on social media?" Here's a hint: share the stuff you've actually created. See why the first 20-minute increment of your Personal Branding Power Hour is so important?

Priority 3– Help other people look good

Why should you spend your time doing this? Because social media is the best means ever invented to say nice things about other people in public. When you spend your time helping other people look good, they'll grow to appreciate you more than you'll ever expect. It also makes you feel good. Why? You need to adopt a grateful mindset to do it.

Trust me on this one. You'll never regret spending the latter part of this 20-minute increment on gratitude.

3rd 20 minutes– Go to School

How much time does the average person spend learning more about their job? If, as reported, over half of Americans read less than five books per year, how valuable will you become if you simply spend 20 minutes each day reading?

What kind of books should you be reading?

Here's a simple thought—ask your customers what books they're reading and start with those. This works great for two reasons:

1. The concepts you learn and verbiage you start using will match that of your customers. The next time someone talks about his or her Hedgehog Concept, you both understand what he or she is saying and are able to add to the conversation.

2. After a customer gives you a book recommendation, they'll love that you actually read it. Why? People love giving advice, but people really love when others actually act on their advice.

Tomorrow, when you spend your first 20-minute increment of your Personal Branding Power Hour writing, you'll have a larger base of knowledge from which to draw.

Just one hour a day keeps anonymity away.

Just imagine if you spend one hour per day—five total hours per week—working on your personal brand through using social media. After spending almost two years of personal trial and error, I'm sharing with you the easiest, most logical way I've found to spend your valuable time on these highly strategic activities.

You may not wish to become a nationally recognized speaker, travelling all over the country meeting people (and new potential customers). But if you do the steps outlined above, you will see real benefits in your professional career—and don't be surprised when they have significant, positive effects on your personal life as well.

Protect your Power Cycle.

Creativity is such an elusive thing. But if you have to 'be creative' as a fundamental part of your 'every day of the week' job, and you're paying attention to the periods when you're most productive (or completely unproductive), you're sure to have noticed a few things about the way you work.

I found this out the hard way very early in my career as an advertising copywriter. Come mid- to late-afternoon, I could wrestle with a problem for literally hours and never come to a satisfactory conclusion. But it never failed—the same vexing issue that eluded me the late afternoon before was solved dead in the first 30 minutes of the next day.

Why? A fresh brain and rested body? A subconscious mind that worked on the problem throughout the night? Just not so tired, hungry and aggravated? Yes, to all of the above, but an even bigger yes to recognizing my personal Power Cycle. There was one insurmountable problem at that job, though. My boss's Power Cycle started at around 7 p.m., and he was a 'nobody leaves before I do' type. Yeah, that didn't last long.

Creative Power Cycles are personal.
And not easily altered.

I didn't waste any time trying to adjust my naturally diurnal cycles to match my boss's nocturnal ones. All that would have gotten me was a lot of physical and mental pain, and a portfolio of crappy work. I got out of that job, learned to recognize and defend my Power Cycle, and was not only a lot happier but more productive too (in both quality and quantity).

As I realized this truth about myself, I started to see it in others as well. My longtime art director *confrere* Wayne Koenig, now a standout UX Lead at Raven Software, is notorious for killing it with amazing work created in the wee hours of the morning. He's naturally nocturnal. I'm naturally diurnal.

We managed to work together seamlessly for a close to a decade—primarily during the periods when our Power Cycles overlapped. We'd disengage, go about our individual roles as required, and then reconvene when necessary, typically when our Power Cycles overlapped again. Is that any way to run a Creative department? Damn right it is, and we have the awards to prove it.

As a Creative Director, I made it a point to determine my team members' individual Power Cycles as quickly as possible—and then schedule things appropriately.

Late afternoon concepting meetings? A complete waste of time. Early morning job starts for my late owl art director? Same thing.

It's not about pandering to the fragile artist and their oh, so precious schedule preferences. It's about getting what you really want: brilliant, creative work.

This is no excuse. It's biology.

The mental effort required to create (not modify, edit, kern, or optimize, etc.) is significant. A writer friend of mine once told me that he believed a focused, bent-on-perfection writer could only effectively write for two hours a day. And I agree.

162

There are outliers, of course. Isaac Asimov is said to have written at least eight hours a day, seven days a week. That worked for him (as one of the most prolific authors in history with over 500 significant published works). But seriously, he's the exception.

Power Cycle: you only get one a day.

For the vast majority of people, there is a single three-to-four-hour period each day that enables the best, most creative, heavy-lift work to happen. I call them 'Power Cycles.' But unlike a machine that once started can keep cranking out work while given enough fuel, the creative engine is susceptible to just about every kind of distraction there is.

To be clear, a huge amount of your daily work will not be spent on 'heavy lift' creativity, and does not require Power Cycle-level energy. Things like billing, conference reports, email processing, appointment coordination, and all the standard TSCODB (time sucking cost of doing business) can and will burn kilowatts of creative energy.

That's why I assign such activity to hours outside my personal Power Cycle. There's no need to waste your best mental energy on a "Sounds good. I'll see you Tuesday" email response when you could use it to solve an intractable creative challenge.

An example that proves the point.

Quality writing consists of three distinct phases:

I. **Conception**
II: **Creation**
III. **Optimization**

The hardest, heaviest lift? **Conception**. The lightest, 'any time of day will do' activity: **Optimization**. And right smack dab in the middle in terms of effort and energy: **Creation**.

Without a **Concept**, the 'what am I actually going to write about,' nothing else can happen. But, for me at least, the second I know the **Concept**, the challenge often shifts to a test of typing speed as the ideas are coming in during the **Creation** phase. While it doesn't require quite the same power level as **Conception**, it's still pretty energy intensive.

Optimization is the phase that finalizes the written product. Spell- and grammar-checking, character or word counting when necessary, editing for clarity and audience—all of these things can be done during those off-Power Cycle hours. It's not that these tasks don't require professional diligence, it's that they don't require **Concept** or even **Creative** energy levels to get the job done well.

What's your species? Know it—and respect it.

So what are you, an up-with-the-sun songbird or an out-all-nite owl? You must recognize and embrace that about yourself. And try to get more specific than that—all the way down to the hours in your 'most productive' window.

It's critically important to know when you are naturally at your creative best—and to then protect that peak period from distractions. During your Power Cycle, don't just ignore email, turn it off. You can deal with all that stuff during off-peak hours, and if they really need you, they'll find others ways to get a hold of you.

Power Cycle scheduling in action.

Let's play out one common scenario: scheduling a meeting. The first step is to understand what the meeting is all about, and its desired outcome or product. Only then can you appropriately schedule for your entire team based on the creative energy level required to achieve that desired outcome.

A weekly status meeting doesn't require much, so schedule it whenever everybody's outside their personal prime time. A big all-call brainstorm that requires the best from everyone? Schedule it for that elusive golden hour when your entire team is ready for prime time.

If you've ever sat in a simple status meeting that happens to be scheduled during your Power Cycle, you really understand what pain is as you can actually feel your Creative energy being wasted.

GTIGCO
(Garbage Time In, Garbage Creative Out)

There are people (typically called 'Managers') who may object to all of this. I can hear them screaming "Yer gettin' paid, so you be creative right now, 'cause I said so."

If you're stuck with someone like that, I feel for you. But if your title is Creative Director, you know that true creativity is a fickle beast. It doesn't come just because you call. It arrives as a lightning bolt to the receptive, searching mind—and more often than not, during that mind's Power Cycle.

Writing quality to garner real ROTOMA?
That's a Power Cycle activity.

If your goal is to create relevant ROTOMA-worthy posts, you best reserve some of your Power Cycle golden hours to write them. Spencer suggests hitting them right at the start of your day, even before office hours when things are quiet and distractions are few. I wholeheartedly agree—unless your Power Cycles start later.

If others are coming in early, there's no problem with you staying late. Again, the goal is quality, not just conventional wisdom regurgitation. Take a common concern or a currently relevant topic, then add your two cents (and more) to write something worth reading, sharing, liking, and subscribing to.

What's your goal?
To have a meeting? Or to have a successful one?

I was once mocked loud & long by an account-side colleague for my 'meeting scheduling *modus operandi*.' It stipulated that 'no significant meetings or presentations happen on Mondays or Fridays, or later than 3 p.m. daily.

But guess what; that strategy worked wonders for the quality of work created, and client acceptance of the work presented, at those meetings.

Why? Power Cycle management. Everyone involved was biologically predestined to perform at their best—and so they did. Clients would arrive rested and receptive. Our team the same. When you purposely remove 'negative biologic universals' like hunger and fatigue from the equation, it's no surprise when the equation leads to a solution everyone can agree with.

Did that mean such significant meetings couldn't occur on Mondays or Fridays? Of course not. True professionals can be called upon to perform with excellence whenever necessary. But if you are setting the meeting and have the choice, schedule your power hitters when they naturally hit most effectively.

Why, oh why, would you ever schedule anything that mattered when everyone in the meeting is not inclined, by simple biology, to give a ... their undivided attention.

As a capital 'C' Creative, the only reason people are going to seek your services is because (surprise) you are CREATIVE. Defend your creativity cubs like a diligent lioness—or watch them, and your work quality and quantity, die.

Unproduction values.

Among the main concerns I hear with clients and prospects in regard to social media are, "How do we know if we're doing the right things? What should we measure? How do we know if we're 'winning'?"

Above all else, I've found one strategy that works with EVERY client, and I'll share that strategy with you shortly. First though, a little background on where this comes from.

When I was just out of college—technically, while I was still in college—I had the good fortune to be hired by IBM. Big Blue describes its three core values as:

- Dedication to every client's success;
- Innovation that matters, for our company and for the world;
- Trust and personal responsibility in all relationships.

My time at IBM taught me that if you have core values, that are written and accepted by fellow IBMers, you'd better live those values. Putting clients first, innovating for the sake of mankind, and trust in all relationships all sound like great aspirations, but I saw them in action every day in our company. In sum, these three core values were both genuine and authentic.

As a result of that experience, I've held IBM and its research in the highest regard. I know the quality of its data is both world class and, more importantly, something from which we can learn and take action.

IBM posed this question to 4,800 CxOs (C-Suite executives):

"What is your biggest barrier to an integrated digital-physical strategy?"

The overwhelming response? **Sixty-three percent said they lack a cohesive social media plan.** What does this tell us? Determining where social media fits in your existing business is really hard. What you say (messaging), where you say it (platform), and how often you share (frequency) are all factors—amongst others—that determine your success. Without a plan, though, how do you know what success really looks like?

Going a step further, if you observe a company actually doing social media well (i.e., large follower counts and high engagement on posts), it may be a little tough to determine why it's actually working. Should you simply emulate what they're doing? What if the techniques they're using are not appropriate for your target audience?

There's one strategy you can implement today that will make things dramatically easier for you; however, like IBM, be genuine and authentic in all things social media.

Most of the emerging social media platforms (like Snapchat), and techniques (like Instagram Stories and Facebook Live) can be summed up in one simple word: **unproduced**.

Instead of content that is highly edited or refined by a graphic designer, users are typically uploading photos or videos directly from their phones with very little concern for lighting, sound quality, or finishing touches.

YouTube has taught anybody paying attention that quality of content trumps quality of production. In fact, in many cases, low production quality creates a sense of *vérité* that makes it feel more *real*.

Not a lot of production value here, but ROTOMA for days.
(Ed. Note: Working out at 4:26 a.m.? Yes, Spencer is 'that guy.')

If any editing is done whatsoever, it will consist of simple captions, a filter to emphasize feeling or highlight a particular location, or even drawings on the screen. Remember, it's not the production that matters—it's the message.

What does the rise of these emerging platforms and techniques tell us? People using these social media platforms desire simple, raw content. They value authenticity first, production-quality second. They want to see if you really are who you say you are.

As an example, I personally advocate that businesspeople like me consider exercising and producing content (writing articles, etc.) first thing in the morning. Before the workday begins, and before things get too hectic, you can create a *Personal Branding Power Hour* (see page 155) to begin your day on a fantastically productive note.

To support my assertions, I provide proof on social media documenting how I actually do these things myself. I take a quick snapshot or video with my phone, share the proof with my audience, and get back to work.

Every one of us with a smartphone currently owns our own media company. At any time, we can show the world what's going on around us, and our audience can share in our experiences. As both an individual and as a representation of your business, what are you sharing with the world?

Do you highlight your outstanding customer service as a component of your business? Prove it. Show your audience that you're practicing what you preach. Do you tout the quality of your products and production process? You don't need a professional film crew to create a documentary. Use the smartphone in your pocket to provide proof now.

Regardless of what social media platforms you use, adopt a culture of genuine, transparent behavior. This mindset will position you as an outlier in the most positive sense possible, and you'll engender trust with your target audience. When developing your social media strategy, start with this word: **authentic.**

In praise of parameters.

As mentioned earlier, if anything is possible, nothing is. Especially for 'Creatives.' A provocative over-statement, perhaps, but it's often true when trying to create work, art, music, poetry, and baked goods.

Endless possibility is often creatively debilitating. I mean, where to start?

For me, it's parameters, as in "let's tightly define the parameters of this project."

Classical poetic forms? **Parameters.**

A cogent Creative Brief? **Parameters.**

.
A stretched canvas? **Parameters.**

Grandma's rye bread recipe? **Parameters.**

Without parameters, there's no wall to push against. No creative handcuffs to overcome. No rules to bend, ignore, or outright break. For art directors and copywriters, there's nothing worse than a Creative Brief that has no defined parameters.

One critical warning:
all parameters are not created equal.
There's always one that dominates all others.
I call this the 'prime parameter.'

An example: a trade show presence.

By its very nature, even with an unlimited budget for creative and execution, there's a prime parameter that absolutely determines what a trade show booth can, and cannot, be: **time**. All other parameters are subservient to this one. And if you think otherwise, you better have a time machine come the night before the show and your booth graphics are "in transit."

As a creative, I have a love / hate /
"please, don't leave me!" relationship
with parameters.

Without them, it's a waste of time to even "get started thinking" about a project. Come back to me when there's a defined budget, timeline, and client-blessed creative brief.

But I also LOVE railing against parameters (e.g., "@#$%%^! If we only had a decent budget / timeline / client /planetary alignment, we could do so much better work!).

Time / Cost / Quality–pick ONE.

You know the old marketing metaphor about the triangle of time, cost, and quality ("Choose two, and we can do it")? Well, it's true—and an attempt to get clients to understand the necessity of defining the project's prime parameter. Even though the metaphor suggests there are two key parameters, in reality, there's only one (and that one has definitive effects the other of the two).

Social media has a number of prime parameters. Twitter's 140-character limit the best example. It's the inverse of *The New York Time's* 'All the News that's Fit to Print' motto. For Twitter, it's "Only the news you can fit." But that's a plus when it comes to ROTOMA. Dashing out a tweet, thumb-typing out a thought while traveling, is easy—and puts you right back at the top of your followers'/customers' minds even while you're at the gate waiting for your flight.

What's your prime parameter?
Define first, then start.

What's your prime parameter? Cost, Time, Quality, Award-winning, Impress my Boss; these are all examples of a prime parameter that creatives can work with. And cheat against. **So figure out your project's prime parameter—then we can all get to work.**

You 'check in.' They check out.

I got an email this week from a salesperson who wants me to do business with his company. In it, he made two major sales mistakes.

1. He started with the subject line of "Checking in."

2. After I responded and said my timeline was at least 120 days, he said, "OK, I'll follow up in four months."

The second mistake is much less obvious. From the salesperson's perspective, he was doing me a service by promising not to bother me until it was time to make a decision. However, from my perspective **he just turned himself into a commodity.**

Guess who's guilty of these same mistakes in the past? Me. Many, many times. Here's what I've learned after being guilty of these errors over many years.

The person you are pitching on any business has a decision process that starts before you make your first pitch and ends when they decide to buy (or not buy). Too many salespeople miss the opportunity to stay connected to their prospects by leveraging social media to provide value during the waiting period.

The person you are pitching continues to live their life while they evaluate your product. That life probably includes research about their company's needs related to your product. It often includes presentations to decision-makers higher up in the company, and hopefully includes some personal trips, milestones, and celebrations.

Social media and email give you the ability to participate in that person's life and become a top-of-mind resource to them—instead of a nuisance—during that decision-making process. If you don't, you'll become "just another salesperson" in their mind.

Shift from 'sales' to 'advisor' mode.

You can save your prospect time during their due diligence effort after your pitch by sending them resources related to your product. Does your organization have white papers explaining the rules, regulations, and challenges of your industry? (If you don't, you should collaborate with your marketing team to create them.)

Have you read an article in a trade publication that made the case for investing in your service or type of product? Send these resources via email to your prospect, giving them useful information and giving them the opportunity to look good by sharing useful resources with their peers and bosses.

You can also continue to stay top of mind with your prospects by **interacting with them in ways that have nothing to do with your product.**

Social media provides you invaluable, near real-time business intelligence about your prospects. By scanning a company's Facebook and LinkedIn pages, you can tell what initiatives they're trying to promote, whether they are expanding or contracting, and you can often read into what immediate challenges they are facing.

Knowledge is power. ROTOMA power.

Armed with this customer intel, it's easy to develop contact points around resources that can help them (rather than sell you).

You might have some insight or another useful white paper about a business challenge they're facing. You can often glean a few personal details, too—birthdays, weddings, childbirth, business trips. If this information has been shared publicly on a social network, it's fair game for you to take action on that information.

If a prospect is traveling to a city that you are familiar with, offer them a restaurant recommendation. If they've celebrated a major personal milestone, send them a snail-mail card offering your congratulations.

To make the sale, stop pitching.

Of course, it should go without saying that the content you share CANNOT be another self-promotional sales pitch. You've already made your pitch. Now you have an opportunity to add value.

One of the best examples of how to add value *after* the sales pitch comes from a winery client my agency has worked with.

Our client needed to find a way to stand out. The world of wine is crowded, and pretty labels may be good in generating one-time transactions but just aren't enough to win customer loyalty. The challenge, then, was how to earn repeat business (loyalty), not just driving trial of the product.

We came up with a solution by putting ourselves in the shoes of the buyer of a bottle.

We asked, "How can we make our customers look good in front of our friends when they serve this wine at a dinner party?" The answer: By equipping the buyer with a story to tell about the wine.

Want customer loyalty?
Tell them a story.

When the customer uncorks the wine, she can tell her guests what to expect in the wine at the first taste, and how that might change as the wine breathes or after she decants it. We tell that story through the message on the label and by continually sharing these stories on social media to generate and build the brand's ROTOMA.

By consciously 'framing' the wine experience *before* they experience it, the brand enables the buyer host to demonstrate expertise and taste. Suddenly, the wine isn't just wine—its a 'make the host look brilliant' tonic. And anytime your buyer feels you make them look smart, that breeds real customer loyalty.

Freely sharing this information in-store and via social media allows our customer to enrich every aspect of her guest experience, making the night more enjoyable and the wine more memorable. And that guests? Don't be surprised when they adopt the wine as their go-to dinner party choice for the very same reasons. They have a story they can tell that generates a wonderful dinner party experience.

Social media and email give you powerful tools to equip your prospects with information that will make their lives easier and make them more valuable to their peers. Why would you ever wait four months between contacting a prospect if you could have been building a relationship and providing them resources and staying top of mind instead?

Master the ABCs, not APPs.

It happened again just as we started writing this book. It occurs so often now, it's become a cliché. A once rapidly rising social media platform—the hyper-locally focused, anonymous chat-oriented Yik Yak—bites the dust. A victim of its own fundamentally flawed service model, the once white-hot tech star (with a reported ~$400 million valuation at its peak) burnt out and was snapped up by Square for just $1 million.

A sad story that serves up a sobering message.

Alas, poor Yik Yak. And Vine, iTunes Ping, Orkut, Xanga, Friendster—you get the drift. Each of these attempts at scalable, sustainable social community building is dead, has pivoted, or relying on deep-pocketed life support. The reasons why are many, varied, and not going to be debated here. But I'd like to make a larger, more personal point: the importance of mastering technique, not the just tools.

The Google giveth.
And the Google taketh away.

I truly believe one thing: if you don't own it, it's not yours. The truth of that statement has been proven over and over again by our search overlords, Google. They more or less killed RSS with Google Reader—and then killed it too. And don't forget other Goognitiatives like Google Video, Google Browser Sync, Google Buzz, plus an entire graveyard full of others.

I'm not saying Google can't or shouldn't shutter whatever they want to, but am trying to make a bigger existential point: Any tool, even ones your career depends on, can be removed from your toolbox at any time (just ask the artists formerly known as Vine Stars.)

Want to build a car?
File a steel bar.

I remember watching a documentary about one of the top German automobile manufacturers (BMW or Mercedes Benz?). It showed how the company onboards new employees: by having them manually file a bar of solid steel—for a solid week. Eight hours a day, with a hand file, trying to get a perfect 90-degree edge on a bar of steel. As I recall, the goal of that kind of 'wax on, wax off' tedium was to impress upon those new employees several things.

1. You have to meet steel where the material lives.

2. You can't force it, but you can shape it.

3. Tools are to be mastered and respected, but are only as good as the hands (and brain) that wields them.

By the end of that week, each new employee develops a cellular-level understanding that there is a right way to do things—and that's what the brand expects.

If you want to work at this highest of tech, I'd argue there's even more to be learned from that story. Things like discipline, diligence, respect for craftsmanship, and attention to detail. But for me, the #1 takeaway was this:

Master the technique, regardless of the tool.

Tools can, and will change, but first principle level techniques (e.g., in cooking; frying, broiling, baking, et al) are forever. Said another way:

Don't confuse technique with software key commands. Key commands change. Techniques don't.

What defines a master carpenter: tools—or technique?

Antonio Stradivari crafted the world's greatest violins with only the most rudimentary of hand tools. Would he be better off with a modern CNC milling machine? I highly doubt it.

The fact is, all the brand and app names mentioned above, and throughout this book, don't matter.

To focus solely on optimizing for 'Social Platform X' is to court your obsolescence. Video did not kill the radio star, just as radio didn't kill live performance, and TV did not kill movies. But not being able to effectively communicate your story? That's career death.

Storytelling transcends channel and platform.

Want to future-proof your career? Learn, and continue to develop, the first principle techniques of your craft, knowing that the key commands will take care of themselves. And never forget, it's all in service to achieving one disciplined goal: telling a story your audience actually wants to engage with.

In other words:
Master your craft's ABCs, and let the APPs take care of themselves.

Making conferences count via savvy social media.

One of my early clients when I started doing social media consulting was a lawyer in Phoenix who concentrated on helping businesses work through mergers and acquisitions. We met up when I was in town for a conference.

"Now that I've made partner, I need to make it rain," he told me. "I'd love to get in front of those businesses that have some kind of financing who are just starting to think about selling in the near future."

The new law partner knew that he wouldn't get a lot of opportunities to run into these kinds of business leaders, since they weren't the types to go to the monthly Chamber of Commerce mixers. He needed to make good on his once-a-year interactions with these entrepreneurs at industry conferences.

The advice I gave him is the advice I give to anyone who doesn't want to be just another face at a conference: Use social media to distinguish yourself before, during, and after the conference.

Here's how to use social media to make the most of those networking opportunities:

Before the conference.

The speakers at industry conferences are great resources with whom to connect. But if you wait until after a speaker gives her talk, you'll probably have to wait in a long line to introduce yourself. Since almost every speaker list is made public before a conference, there's no reason to wait until the conference to connect with these influencers.

Research conference speakers on social media, connect with them on LinkedIn (send a note providing context, of course), and then start posting about those speakers on your channels. Tag them, like them, and promote them to your audiences. Those speakers will notice, and they may even seek you out at the conference. At the very least, they'll be more likely to recognize your name.

If you're someone who likes to prepare for conferences by doing some research on the attendees and speakers so you know who to seek out during networking breaks, then this should come naturally to you. The research is an easy task to delegate to a personal assistant, and the posts take only a few minutes to create.

At the conference.

If you want people to remember you after the conference, there are two things you should do while you're there. (Obviously, this is in addition to introducing yourself to the people you researched and connected with ahead of time.)

Bryan Cook was definitely worth meeting—
and remembering.

1. Take a picture with the people you want to remember—and you want to remember you.

That's quite a sentence, but so true. If you meet someone and you have an enjoyable conversation that you think could one day lead to a business relationship, ask him or her to take a photo with you. It will help you remember who you met and when, let's face it, a week after a conference it's hard to distinguish the people you talked to and what the conversations were, and it will be useful for conference follow-up.

2. Live tweet the conference.

You may be thinking, "Nobody really reads conference Twitter hashtags, except the conference organizers."

... except the conference organizers.

If you want to make an impression on the conference organizers, who are likely influencers in your industry, show them some love on Twitter. Since conference hashtags are woefully underused, if you tweet three or four times during each session you attend, you'll likely draw the attention of the conference chair, who is probably also the person in charge of booking speakers for the next year.

Conference organizers are an important audience.
You scratch their back, maybe they'll scratch yours.

Sometimes when we plan out our social media activity, we get obsessed with trying to optimize our activity to get the most number of views or the highest engagement.

But if you're strategic about it, that one view on social media may be the only one you need.

After the conference.

Before the conference high wears off—during that one-week honeymoon period—be sure to follow-up with all of your new connections. This is a great time to post those photos you took with the people you met, especially on LinkedIn because of its business-focused nature. Tag them and introduce them to your network, while sharing something about their work that will be relevant and provide value to your audience.

Then, put a note in your calendar to check in on these connections in three months, and six months, and nine months.

Finally, put a Google Alert on the company or the individual's name. If they get good press, you should be the first one sharing their stories and promoting their achievements.

Being active on social media should never replace getting out in the community and meeting the doers in your industry, but it's an excellent supplement. Used strategically, social media can help you maximize the time and effort you put into growing your network and will provide you with influence long after the in-person meetings.

Remember: the time to strategize your conference ROTOMA activity is well in advance of any event.

The planning you do now will make actually executing the plan at the conference possible. Here are some pre-conference tips that can really max out your ROTOMA before, during, and after the event.

Pre-Conference ROTOMA Checklist

☐ Make a 'Meet' List of people you're going to make a concerted effort to meet, greet, and *Unselfishly Selfie* with (see D.P.'s concept in the next section).

☐ Create a personal show hashtag and start using it in the weeks before the event (as well as during and after the event.) Example: #CUatNAMM2018.

☐ Who doesn't want a photo of themselves? Make sure to instantly copy the photos you just took to all the people in it, and in order to maximize your ROTOMA, do it via social media.

To do so, you'll need their Twitter handles, so be sure to ask for them at the time if you haven't already determined them as part of your pre-conference reconnaissance.

If you only embrace one technique from this book, steal this one. It's a really smart, stealthy way to grow your ROTOMA contact list.

☐ Take a few minutes to retweet conference photos as they happen. Be sure to include the relevant hashtags for maximum effect (e.g., #NAMM2018, #CUatNAMM2018, et al).

Unselfish Selfies.

I continue to learn a lot about how to work the levers of social media simply by watching the master at work. Spencer's the man when it comes to all this stuff, and understanding and implementing the many techniques and posting styles he uses to fill his feeds is imperative to max out your ROTOMA potential.

Seriously, the dude does not quit—and hasn't met a name he couldn't drop. This simple picture says a heck of a lot more than the few accompanying words attached to it.

It's not just self-promotion when you're sharing and promoting others.
Really smart point, Spencer.
And yes, I know it's not technically a selfie.

Here's how I break it down:

A. Here I am, Spencer, at a major 'thought leaderish' event. Since I'm attending, that makes me a 'thought leader'.

B. I legitimately praise the speaker, mentioning that I am a longtime reader of one of the world's leading publications for startups and agility-oriented companies. Once again, that implies that I am a citizen of the Fast Company startup and agility-oriented business universe.

C. I'm happily promoting the multi-day conference on day one, thereby making this a valuable promotional shoutout for the conference #WITreps.

D. The name pile-on at the end? That's a bunch of folks I met at the conference who might like (literally) any number of things about this photos, such as:

>A. I liked because I attended the same event;

>B. I liked the keynote;

>C. I like Alan Webber;

>D. I like Fast Company magazine;

>E. I am a citizen of the FC business universe;

>F. I like that Spencer gave me/people I recognize or follow a shoutout for being a 'thought leader;'

>G. I like seeing myself (and others I recognize or follow) recognized for any reason;

>H. Spencer always likes my posts, and I reciprocate right back.

And the list could go on for a lot longer. 21 people (including Spencer) are mentioned in that post, and it already received 23 likes within the first three hours—and while the conference was still in session.

Now that's not Kim Kardashian-level liking, but then Spencer's no KK (sorry dude, truth hurts). But it's pretty good for under 3 hours on LinkedIn, especially given the subject matter.

Minimal effort. Maximal effect.

So how much time did it take Spencer to get, process and post this to LinkedIn? I'm guessing minutes—maybe 10 at most. And yet the networking and personal-brand promoting effect of those ten minutes is surely worth far more.

Spencer effectively promoted:

1. The speaker;

2. The conference and its organizers;

3. All the conference's sponsors;

4. The attendees;

5. The topic;

6. The city of Madison as a top-tier innovation center;

7. And only after all that, himself.

That is what I call an 'unselfish selfie,' and as Spencer points out in *Make Conferences Count* on page 183, it's one of the easiest ways to fill your feeds with sharing, value, and laser-focused, relevant personal and professional promotion. If you ask me, that's doing social—smart.

World Class ROTOMA– a Master Class.

You know what a 'tell' is? Originating in the game of poker, a 'tell' is an involuntary physical response or 'tic' that effectively tells the other players that you're bluffing. Well, I've got a personal 'tell' to tell you about.

If you ever see the words 'world class' in the copy I write, it's a near perfect indicator that I do not have anything meaningful to say. It's pure fluff, designed to flesh out a sentence or paragraph. It's the linguistic equivalent of air in a box.

But not this time.

Remember my friend Nicole, the maternity and newborn photographer in Minnesota (see *What's your Flagship,* page 77)? When I say she's a world class photographer in her genre, I'm not kidding. I can prove she is very simply. She's 'world class' because the World says so— via Instagram.

Moscow? *You're doing a workshop in Moscow?*

London too? WTFabulous!

Nicole, I hate you. ;)

Seriously, if I didn't know how hard she's worked to achieve this kind of ROTOMA, I would be a raging, green-eyed envy machine. But I'm not, because I do know how much blood, literal sweat, and 'am I doing this right' tears went into building her personal and professional brand.

You want to see her entire ROTOMA strategy in action? Check out her Instagram feed from her very first post to today. She's given me permission to do this, so don't feel weird—after all this is exactly the kind of personal bread crumb trail you are leaving all over the 'Net. Not comfortable with the heat in the kitchen? Get out (but that also means you don't get any of the goodies being active in the kitchen supplies).

Nicole's very first Instagram post: 11.5.2011

OK, this is hilarious. Her first post is the biggest social media cliché there is: a picture of the lunch she was eating. BWAHAHAHAHAHA!

But that makes sense. Nicole, like all of us in those days, was trying to figure out how this new channel could possibly work for her. Sharing a good looking food shot? Why not—I've seen other people do it.

At the beginning, her Insta-feed was nothing but the usual stuff: family photos, pics of events she attended, the occasional 'look where we went' archival image. But slowly, and after a false start or two, it began morphing into something else: the flagship social media channel for her brand, Charlie & Violet Photography. And that's when it started to take off.

First post as Charlie & Violet Photography 5.11.2014

20 likes. Not bad for a brand new Insta-business.

Fast forward to July 14, 2017

1,231 Likes and climbing for a solo-entrepreneur?
Yeah, I'll take that.

1,231 Likes from all over the globe.

Those Likes come from all over the world. And some of them are going further and inviting her to take her workshop show on the road to their part of the globe. And the rubles the Russians paid to get her there? Let's just say they Любите ее большое время.

Need to quantize ROTOMA?
How's that for starters.

Go to Nicole's Instagram feed, start at the very first posts at the bottom, then scroll up. You can literally see her develop as not only an artist and photographer but as a badass businesswoman.

I remember when she started this exciting act in her life (after years of being a standout art director at traditional ad agencies). She called me up to tap my brain for promotional concepts on how to get people to actually book her for sessions.

I gave her a few ideas but am sad to say using Instagram as a social media flagship for demonstration, sharing, and eventually hard-ask sales was not one of them. But boy, how I learned the power of Instagram simply by watching her go.

With social media, the world is your oyster (and potential customer, colleague, and friend).

Any stamp collectors out there anymore? Probably not, or certainly not as many as there just a few decades ago. I remember hearing (or maybe watching) a story about an older man who for years was fascinated with three words: Tristan de Cunha.

If I remember correctly, as a boy he stumbled across a postage stamp labeled with the name of this incredibly exotic place. That chance exposure lead to a lifetime of fascination for this incredibly remote island nation in the south Atlantic Ocean.

With a population of just 252 (2017 estimate, thanks Wikipedia), this member of the British Commonwealth is the remotest inhabited island on earth. And Twitter's giving me the venue to explore this fascinating place via social media.

D.P. Knudten
@dpknudten

Any Tristan de Cunhaians on Twitter? If so, please respond if you're interested in having a Twitter pen pal in the U.S.A. #tristandecunha

Jul 19 2:20 PM

0 RETWEETS   0 LIKES

Ask and ye may receive—courtesy of Twitter.

I haven't heard anything back yet, but I am confident the power of social media will rectify this situation soon. And this is the kind of outreach and connection social media affords—at absolutely no cost to you.

What was impossible is now mundane.

What formerly only nation states and global institutions could do, you can at any time of the day or night, and anywhere you happen to be *via your phone*.

The only barrier to entry in this market is your attitude.

**It literally doesn't get any easier than this.
So grab your mobile, and start now!**

ROTOMA / NOW

Alright, you get it.

The why, where, what, and how of ROTOMA.

Now it's your turn.

Get your voice, vision, experience, and expertise out there.

So what are you waiting for?

GO!

Perfect practice.

As a 'live and let live' kind of place, the state of Wisconsin requires very few things of its citizens. A love of cheese and beer. The tolerance of a summer-long invasion from broad-shouldered Illini. And a cellular-level reverence for the Green Bay Packers, and the team's 'deity who walked among us' Coach Vince Lombardi.

The dude knew what he was talking about when it comes to performing at your very best. And he understood exactly what it takes to succeed.

> *"Practice does not make perfect.*
> *Only perfect practice makes perfect."*
> - Vince Lombardi

You can, and should, apply this wisdom to your ROTOMA efforts without fail. As stated several times throughout this book, **if you want the outcome, you have to put in the work**. But, IMHO, it should all be based on a disciplined foundation focused on the fundamentals.

What are your fundamentals?

Facebook, LinkedIn, Twitter, Instagram, YouTube, Snapchat, blogging, 'whatever the next big social media thing is': You can't do everything. What should you do? That's question #1, which Spencer and I have tried to address throughout this book.

But an actually more important question is what *can* and *will* you do to receive the real personal and career benefits of ROTOMA? Answer those questions, and you have defined your fundamentals.

I'm not a sports-guy myself, but I completely understand the constant coaching reminder to 'stick to the fundamentals.' These are the very basic level activities and practices that allow you to achieve the higher level goals you seek.

For football players, it's blocking and tackling, passing and running.

For musicians, it's warming up with scales and standard arpeggios.

For ballet dancers, it's starting with a regime of barre exercises that prepare the body to perform at its best.

And for social media, it's creating a daily schedule and sticking to it, whether you like it or not.

Waiting for inspiration leads to exactly one thing: *waiting*.

Good writers know one thing for rock solid certain. The only cure for writer's block is writing. Or in my case, typing. There's something about lining up my fingers on the home row keys (asdf and jkl;) that shifts my mind into gear.

A lot of times, it's a low-power, barely moving first gear, but at least it's forward movement of some sort. And the 'delete' key gets more use than any other for a while. **But then it strikes: inspiration.** Is that what Louis Pasteur meant when he said "…chance favors only the prepared mind."? I think so.

Not every post is going to earn an A+. ROTOMA says "So what?"

Ever get poked on Facebook? All this dorky little feature, this inane snippet of code does is allow someone in your FB network to give you a virtual nudge (or you, them). You receive notification that 'so and so' poked you. It's stupid. And I love it.

The intellectual content of a poke is next to nothing—but it isn't nothing. And the really funny thing? That stupid little act is more or less the primary channel of communication between me and a beloved former colleague of mine who moved away.

She'll send me a poke. I'd smile and send her one back. And that's it, except for one 'entirely germane to this book' point:

**With that stupid little poke,
she jumps to the very top of my mind for a while
after dropping completely off it over time.
*That is ROTOMA in action.***

Vince was right.

Perfect practice does makes perfect. So what's your ROTOMA 'perfect practice' today? It could be the religious observance of Spencer's 'Personal Branding Power Hour' routine (*Personal Branding Power Hour* page 155).

It could be as simple as Liking whatever you find on LinkedIn over lunch. Simply adding a brief comment to that Like and you've just boosted your ROTOMA quotient significantly.

Attending a professional event, a client's Grand Opening, an internal awards presentation? Instagram (and Facebook, LinkedIn, Twitter) pics of you and your crew with appropriate @ tagging, and you've just multiplied your ROTOMA like a boss.

You can do it. Start now.

How? Here's a starter post to get you going. It's a bit gratuitous, I admit, but my ROTOMA shame knows no bounds (and neither should yours). Here's what I'd LOVE for to do:

1. Get out your phone.

2. Take a quick photo of the cover of this book.

3. Open up your Flagship app (see *What's your Flagship,* page 77)

4. Type in the following (or whatever you wish):

"Just finished #ROTOMA. Spencer had really great ideas re: social media. D.P., not so much, but he's dead sexy. @spencerXsays @dpknudten"

5. Post it. I guarantee you'll get at least two Likes & Follows (from guess who).

6. You are now officially ROTOMA certified. It's up to you to take it from here. Good luck!

— D.P. Knudten

PS: I'd like to personally invite you to become a citizen of the ROTOMA Universe. Spencer and I have big plans for it, but it all starts by offering you FREE downloadable worksheets, special deals, and exclusive web-based content at **rotomathebook.com**. *Be sure to check back often as we'll be adding even more over time. ROTOMA is a big idea, and we'd love for you to become an equally big part of it. - dp*

The Salesman's Mistake doesn't have to be yours.

Between the years of 2008 and 2015, I did about 3,000 in-person sales meetings. Learned a lot? Yes, I did, and I've shared a lot of it here with you.

I'd like to end with an old sales adage—and warning:

**Beware of things that work so well,
you stop doing them.**

You may say that sounds kind of silly. The reality is quite simple. After all of these sales meetings, I started to get bored. So eventually I started thinking "I should probably change this up and try something else to keep myself entertained." And that is a critical mistake.

D.P. once told me there's a similar truism in advertising: that if you're bored of your campaign, that means it's just getting noticed.

That's probably what's going on at your business right now. You're providing some kind of benefit that's free or low-cost that can really help get people in the door, and you're simply not amplifying it because you think to yourself, "Doesn't everybody know that we do this?" The answer is no.

So, next time you're wondering, "What should I be sharing on social media?" look at the things around you that you are already providing as a benefit, the things that are old hat to you, but highly beneficial to your clients, and turn it into a social media post that says "Hey, this is something that you can take advantage of right now."

An example: what's the most famous painting in the world? You likely said Da Vinci's Mona Lisa. But what's the most famous Farmer's Market in the world? If you live in Madison where I do, it's the fantastic Farmer's Market that surrounds the Capitol Building every summer Saturday. Was that your answer? Probably not, as it relies on a lot of variables, not the least of which is where you live.

My point? That you don't have to be the most famous person in the world, but it's doesn't hurt to be well-known to those within your personal and professional universe. You don't have to be known and respected by everyone online, just those within your sphere of influence. And the real power of ROTOMA is in extending that sphere over time.

Write, curate, share, and promote what you know to the people you know. If it's relevant, they'll take it from there, enlarging your sphere of social influence every day.

My final encouragement, be mercilessly consistent. As D.P. is fond of saying (perhaps from reading all those Patrick O'Brien books) 'Stay the course.' Repetition breeds results—especially when it comes to social media.

Need help getting started?
Check out **rotomathebook.com**

This book is just the beginning of something much bigger. I encourage you to become part of it by visiting **rotomathebook.com** for FREE downloadable content, worksheets, and most importantly, encouragement. After all, the only person who is *guaranteed* to receive no benefit from social media is the one not doing it.

Don't let that person be you.

- Spencer X. Smith

Spencer X. Smith & D.P. Knudten

Thanks.

This book was the result of the help and active encouragement of a lot of people, professional and personal. Spencer and I would love to wax on about their many contributions, but since that would require another book-length section, this simple list will have to suffice. The order is alphabetical because there is no other way to prioritize the names when in reality all of them deserve a place at the top of the list.

Brian Solis / briansolis.com
Bryan Cook
Darin Tessier
Diana Pastrana
Eric S. Yuan / CEO, Zoom
Erica 'The Comma' Smith
Erin Ogden / OgdenGlazer, LLC
Grant Baldwin / *The Speaker Lab* podcast
Harriet Hritz
Hilary Meyerson / Little Candle Media
JESS3 / jess3.com
Jlyne Hanback
John Bohlinger / *Premier Guitar*
Jon Levy / *Premier Guitar*
Jillian Carroll
Judy Firek
Katie George / @katiecosplays
Melanie Deziel / mdeziel.com
Mona Preece-Davis / ClosetMaid
Nick Lombardino
Nicole Klein / Charlie & Violet Photography
Professor Scott Galloway / NYU Stern School of Business
Rachel Neill / Carex Consulting
Ruth Soukup / livingwellspendingless.com
Sandra Long / Post Road Consulting
Stephanie Larson / AmpliPhi
Wayne 'Dragon' Koenig
Workfront
Zoom

Spencer X. Smith & D.P. Knudten

Spencer X. Smith

Spencer Smith is the founder of spencerXsmith.com, an Instructor at the University of Wisconsin, and Adjunct Faculty at Rutgers University, where he teaches classes on Social Media Strategy. After working as both a Regional Sales Director and Regional Vice President for two Fortune 100 companies, Spencer is now sharing his ROTOMA experience & stories with those who could benefit from his 3,000+ in-person business development meetings.

He's been called a "Digital Marketing Expert" by *Forbes*, and is the winner of the 2016 *InBusiness* Magazine Executive Choice Award for Social Media Consulting Company. Spencer also co-founded social media marketing company AmpliPhi in 2017, and specializes in providing Business Generation Solutions for Modern Companies. Spencer speaks at an average of 60 conferences and other events per year, and only teaches what he first has proven to work himself with his own business. For more details, visit spencerXsmith.com/ROTOMA

@spencerXsays

spencerxsmith

@spencerXsmith

sxs@spencerXsmith.com

spencerXsmith.com/ROTOMA

D.P. Knudten

D.P.'s advertising and marketing career has included some of the biggest, and smallest, brands in the business including Coca-Cola, The Athlete's Foot, ClosetMaid—and Southeastern Guide Dogs. His career includes stints at DDB Needham/Chicago and McCann Erickson/Atlanta and ad agencies in Denver, Madison, and Sarasota. As a longtime copywriter and Creative Director, he enjoys playing in the creative intersection between the visual and the verbal—and has actually gotten paid to do so for over a quarter century.

D.P. is currently the owner and Chief Collaborator of COLLABORATOR creative, a content marketing firm specializing his NonFiction Branding™ approach to identifying, creating, and amplifying the true brand stories of individuals and companies throughout the United States. He speaks frequently about this, ROTOMA, a variety of other topics to groups nationwide. For more details, visit collaboratorcreative.com/speaking

𝕏 @dpknudten

in dpknudten

f @dpknudten

✉ dp@dpknudten.com

🏠 collaboratorcreative.com

Made in the USA
Lexington, KY
31 January 2018